1

Naughty Jak
The Story of a Difficult Puppy

By

*ABL*ang

Naughty Jak
The Story of a Difficult Puppy

First Printing, 2020

Dedication

This book is dedicated to the memory of

Twixiferalius Wakadoodle Teabag Hobo Mischief Barnett Lang Simpkins

Without whom this story would not have ever begun.

Table of Contents

Foreword

I first met Jak and Barbara on Friday 7th June 2019. It was a hot summer afternoon and I remember feeling intrigued as to what I would find when I arrived.

Barbara had given me a brief overview of what to expect, but I don't think I was at all prepared for the tornado that was Jak!

To this day, Jak remains one of the most complex and anxious dogs I have ever met. His anxiety manifested in many different ways, none of which were pretty. Barbara, understandably, had reached the end of her wit and was noticeably stressed and frustrated. Here's the thing though, stressed and frustrated human plus anxious and over aroused dog, is not a good mix. The whole partnership was doomed if drastic changes weren't made very quickly.

Made they were! I want to thank you, Barbara, for being so open-minded throughout the whole process and for allowing me to think outside of my toolbox in order to crack this case.

Ultimately, the changes made and the hard work put in have turned Jak, the dangerous tornado into Jak, a truly beautiful dog. It was my pleasure to work with you both and I wish you every success moving forward.

Hannah Price

Head Trainer, Canissimo Dog Training

Note from the Author

What this book is..

This book is the story of two great friends. Barbara and Katy, living in a season of family changes and lifestyle challenges, who work together to bring up a crazy, difficult and very reactive Red Collie called Jak. Jak's full name is Kaiser Jackaroo Scooby Tigger Bandicoot Rebel Redboy III. (In our family pets get new names added to their name as new character traits emerge over time)!

This book has been written from excerpts of real emails and records of real conversations that took place over the period of eighteen months starting in September 2018. The recounting of training sessions are accurate as are the descriptions of incidents and accidents taking place within the life of Jak.

This book aims to encourage puppy and young dog owners who feel that they cannot cope or that life will never be any better.

What this book is not…

This book is not a recommendation of training methods. If anything the journey I have taken with Jak has shown me that even knowing lots of training techniques does not ensure any forward trajectory on the 'good behaviour' scale.

Through my avid reading of any dog books I could get access to I have amassed a vast knowledge of different ways to train dogs. I have also seen that, just with Jak, I have had to use different techniques at different stages of Jak's development and even on different days depending on Jak's state of mind and anxiety levels.

Therefore, this book does not claim to endorse any particular type of training nor ages at which these methods will be successful.

It is important to state that if you are having any symptoms of aggression with a dog you do need to consult urgently with a behavioural specialist. Please do not put yourself, or others, in any danger of aggressive behaviour, especially if you do not understand what is causing it. Professional help is essential.

Acknowledgements

Firstly, I would like to thank Katy, who has been a daily support through the difficult journey of wild Collie ownership that I embarked on in October 2018.

I especially wish to thank her for reading my long email mutterings of despair, doom and gloom so numerous that they took an entire day to copy and paste into the rough outline for this manuscript! I also thank Katy for the timely messages of hope and thoughts for my well-being and the health and happiness of my family.

I also acknowledge the long months where I have been mentally absent from my family, as a wife and mother, whilst I have been busy reading yet another 'How to' dog book or searching frantically online to find the solution to a new problem that Jak had presented our family with.

I want to show appreciation to each family member, whether living in my home, elsewhere in the United Kingdom, or in South Africa for their patience with me through this traumatic time which has not as yet concluded with a happy and relaxed family dog!

I would also like to thank the many Dog Trainers who have helped me, both in face to face training sessions, and online or over the telephone.

Every trainer, at each stage, has input into Jak's journey and I think of you all with gratitude when I am using the techniques you took the time to teach me. Thank you.

Prologue: A life that needed changing

Throughout the spring and summer of 2018 my life was in a turmoil. I was struggling with the pressure of my work as a Minister of Religion. I was starting to feel old and despite being a lifelong outdoors addict I was spending far too much time indoors. Too much time being bored in the evenings and in the early morning. Too much time alone. No new project on the horizon and the years stretching in front of me to my retirement date looked drear and unexciting.

In addition, I had been living with two elderly dogs belonging to my older children who had left home. Jessie a golden, although now shades of white, Cocker Spaniel who spent many hours of each day sleeping on her back with her legs in the air noisily dreaming of the type of rabbit chasing that her poor displaced hips would never permit. And Twix a tiny, slightly non-descript cross between a Maltese Poodle and a Miniature Pinscher (allegedly).

Twix lived a busy life with a constant patter of tiny paws and clatter of tiny claws on hard floors tick tick tacking along observing everything that was going on day and night.

In comparison Jessie lived a more placid life just sleeping in front of her radiator and constantly crying at food time or walk time. Both dogs were born in South Africa and migrated across the continents at about age six or seven. It was Twix, though, who won my heart completely and is really where this story begins.

Whilst Twix was waiting for my daughter Milly, his real mother, to buy a property where pets were allowed Twix slept in his bed next to my bed. Twix could not be contained, he was most indignant when zipped up in his travel crate, either at night time or when we had tradesmen visiting.

When I returned home, from even the shortest absence, on opening the front door, I would hear Twix tick ticking from wherever he was in the house running to greet me and being oh so happy that I was home.

I was very keen for Twix and Milly to be reunited and together with Milly's husband Axcle I knew it would be a happy life for them all. However as the purchase of the property loomed and the date of Twix leaving me grew ever nearer, I started to feel a worry about coming home to a house without Twix, waking up to a morning without Twix. What would it be like? How would I feel? Would I cope? The questions flew around my head like machine gun fire. I had to do something.....but what?

It did occur to me that with only having one elderly dog in the house, perhaps now would be the perfect time for a puppy?

Of course, this thought could have ended with me picturing a tiny mini Twix sized puppy arriving and becoming part of my life and that of my family. However, with my strong desire to be outdoors so much more at this time my head took me down a completely different path!

Katy, my best friend of many years, chatted to me as I wrestled with these seemingly impossible problems of life. Her advice was simple..."Get a Collie" she said, "Life will never be the same".

So on the 6th October 2018 I got a Collie......and I can truly say: "Life was never the same again!"

Baby Jak

I spent many happy hours daydreaming about my own Collie and researching the breed. I learnt so much about these clever and faithful dogs. I could picture my new friend beside me, hiking and camping together, as I read about collies and puppies. Then the searching for a breeder and a puppy began. I searched the internet ceaselessly for at least four weeks phoning and messaging possible breeders to find out more. It took a while to decide exactly what type of puppy I wanted most.

Katy owned a beautifully marked black and white Border Collie called Mizzle who was now around five years old. Capable and clever she lived up to her good pedigree background. It would have been possible for me to look at breeders owning dams from the same bloodlines as Mizzle. Surely that would have been the most sensible option?

In my life's history I have rarely taken the easiest or most sensible route to anywhere and this decision was to be no different. In my mind's eye I could not see myself with a black and white dog and where Mizzle was slim delicate and very pretty looking I thought that I liked my dogs to look a bit more rough and ready.

Of course I knew I wanted a clever puppy. After all, I was going to teach it every trick I could think of. As I preferred the Collies with brown and white markings, I began to read up about both purebred Welsh Sheepdogs and Welsh Collies, sheepdogs who had some Border Collie in their heritage.

I loved the look of them in pictures but all articles were suggesting that Welsh Sheepdogs always belong on a farm and even Welsh Collies may require more attention than Border Collies. There were several Facebook pages dedicated to Welsh Collies where owners have uploaded photos of happy Welsh Collies and pups who look adorable and completely happy.

Evidently I should perhaps have thought long and hard about the fact that one photo is a mere two second glimpse into the life of the dog and family, not a true representation of twenty four hours day after day!

This was a fact that I obviously chose not to linger on as I had made up my mind as to how the future looked.......and of course I had successfully trained several dogs throughout my life. I could totally make this work.

Finally, I was in discussion with a lady who had a litter of Collie puppies. The sire was a huge red aristocratic looking Collie, I couldn't stop looking at his beautiful picture, and the dam was a black and white Collie. Both parents lived with the breeder and could be seen. The location of the litter was in Merthyr Tydfil, Wales. The Breeder ran a training school there and, after several emails, I felt certain that this puppy would have had a great start. The puppies had had lots of early training and sound desensitization and so on. To my eyes, the sire looked a bit more like a Welsh type Collie than a Border Collie. This made me a little bit nervous. However, there was one red boy unreserved that I could go and view. My heart leapt.

The puppy was going to be ready to leave the litter on the sixth of October which fitted in perfectly with my plans. Twix was due to leave us on the 4th October.

So I drove to Wales to view the parents and the puppies who were at this point about four weeks old. I noticed that the Sire seemed a bit hyperactive and maybe even unruly (but what did I know?). He looked very happy though leaping around with the toys from the puppy's pen.

I asked practical questions about the parents and the litter and discussed the prospective lifestyle I was planning for the puppy. The breeder took me to the barn where the puppies were living. I was holding my breath with excitement. When the six puppies ran out of their pen they were, of course, gorgeous.

The little red boy was a bit plumper than his littermates. He followed behind them hoovering up any bits of food he found. The Breeder was keen to show me that the puppies were comfortable with the other animals that lived in the barn. A good menagerie! So the puppies were encouraged to explore the stalls inside the barn.

As the litter ran into the sow's pen in the corner of the barn the pups all climbed over the sow except the plump red pup, he sneaked into the pen and started cautiously eating out of the sow's food bowl. It worried me for a second, then I reassured myself when I remembered that puppies who are food motivated can be more easily trained.

When the breeder picked up the plump red puppy, he nuzzled into her neck and licked and licked. I thought it was adorable, how I longed for that to be me cuddling and snuggling with my new puppy. It did not occur to me on that day, or subsequently, that excessive licking may be a sign of possible submissive behaviour. I was very keen to pay my deposit and drove home singing.

Finally, my life was coming together. I needed this. I had already decided to call my new puppy Jak short for Jackeroo, an apprentice worker with sheep and cattle. Obviously Jak was going to learn lots and lots from being with me!

It was very difficult to wait for the few weeks before Jak was old enough to be collected. The breeder was very helpful sending updates on the socialisation that the litter had experienced and many details of my puppy's first things. Some of the very earliest photos I have came from the breeder before Jak was the statutory eight weeks old.

I drove to Merthyr Tydfil by myself to pick up Jak. Jak was going to be my dog, my responsibility, I wanted to do this for myself. I had brought a travel crate and a cuddly toy, towels and blankets. I was imagining a long drive home with the occasional barking or whimpering session. How wrong I was. Jak barked and howled for the entire journey other than when the car was stationary at traffic lights. It was not a good beginning.

I do see now that I should have arranged someone to drive me home so that I could have perhaps held Jak or his travel crate on my lap and talked to him to comfort him. Would it have made a huge difference to all that was to follow? Looking back at the months that followed this I doubted it.

When we got home I noticed straight away just how big Jak's paws were. I remembered Mizzle's neat legs and pretty paws and wondered about Jak's thumping big ones. Still, I had particularly chosen a dog with no pedigree. I knew there was no guarantee of his heritage.

Just a week or so after I was finding life with Jak very enjoyable. Jak was a real cutie. We loved hanging out in the garden together. Jak was fairly calm other than his after breakfast chaotic moment and his after supper chaotic run about. Jak did, already, get super excited when he saw people and sometimes he had a small accident in those moments but otherwise he was really clean in the house.

I found that doing usual things like keeping the house tidy and so on were impossible due to the amount of my time that Jak now took up. Any sense of routine had gone out of the windo. Katy helped me with tactics to help reduce the over excited wetting, suggesting trying to ignore Jak or for us to turn our backs when he greeted us. It did work to a certain degree. Katy's advice regarding housework and routines was to forget worrying about those things until Jak was having long and tiring walks. All would settle down then she was sure.

I could hardly wait. I so loved walking with a dog and I could picture Jak and I out miles from home just walking. Katy also encouraged me to make sure I enjoyed the puppy bit remembering that it doesn't last long.

Well that all sounded good! But I may have to go back to Katy now that it is eighteen months after this particular advice to say "err Katy I'm still wrestling with the puppy bit"!

Toys and Games

Before the end of October, I had decided that Jak was more clever than me. I had been trying to teach him to fetch the tennis ball, which is a favourite game of Mizzle's. But Jak always ran for the ball and then didn't quite bring it back. Often he just ran away with it. It quickly became a game that Jak was in charge of and it remains one of his most favourite games of all time.

The game is "I have something you want, I show you and I run away with it time and time again" mixed in with the game of "You can't catch me". The fact that we were not getting anything like a retrieve or on going game at all made me choose to put the tennis ball away until Jak was older. There was the odd time that we tried the game again like the day that my sister in law, Beryl and six year old nephew, Marcus visited. They brought Jak a pack of three fancy branded rubber squeaky balls. I tried playing with Jak with one of those. These different balls, then, were Jak's ball rather than the tennis ball that belonged to me that I kept safe when we were not playing. Many puppy books had recommended that the owner instigating and ending games was a good way to show leadership. I am not sure that Jak noticed.

Jak did actually fetch the new ball back very expertly a few times before he suddenly ran off with it. This proved to me that Jak not only understood the "Fetch the ball" game and could play it, but that he was choosing to play it by his own rules. On thinking about all this later I was not quite sure if Jak was training me, rather than me training him. A problem I would encounter often!

Katy was very encouraging. Reminding me how clever Jak was and how eventually we would get the fetch game sorted. But I was not so sure.

One morning when it was cold and frosty outside and I was in the garden with Jak I was wearing a treasured navy blue knitted beanie hat. As I bent down to pick up the ball to throw for Jak he snatched the hat off my head and ran off with it. Amazingly, I could not get it back at all. I could not catch Jak, I could not outwit him and he teased me by dropping it near me and then snatching it seconds before I could put my hand on it. This continued for a long time and the hat was never the same again.

We had lots of fun when Jak was tiny playing outside together and training inside. Jak and I loved spending time together and I loved day dreaming about all the things we would be able to do together.

One of my own thoughts about owning a Collie had been an interest in herding. I grew up watching 'One Man and his Dog' on television and thought it all looked really great. I had no idea if I would be up for it or if Jak would but I knew that I would want to find out if my Collie could herd.

Having allowed Jak to play outdoors with my nephew, Marcus, I felt that I no longer needed to worry about Jak not having the ability to herd. As Marcus ran around the garden incessantly Jak was most definitely watching, positioning himself and at times lying down just watching intently. So it was all good there. I just needed to find out if Jak was interested in working with sheep, or indeed, if I had any sheep herding aptitude.

Jak grew physically very quickly. He doubled in size in the first two and a half weeks he was with me. Jak was very unsettled though, every day. After a few days of really unsettled behavior I decided to increase the amount of kibble in Jak's meals measuring his adult weight on the puppy food sack as 30kg for a male Welsh Sheepdog rather than 25kg for a male Border Collie because of those huge paws and legs. This did seem to help settle him a bit.

Still, having had several different breeds of puppies before, and being used to a play, play, play sleep, sleep, sleep routine I was starting to get concerned that Jak never slept unless he was shut in his crate.

The longer I kept him out of his crate, the more he would potter, chew and run around until he was so over tired that he was nipping, biting, barking and generally being really badly behaved. Once in his crate, which was covered with a blanket, Jak slept soundly until we opened the crate again when 'game on' restarted.

This pattern continued until the present day. No sleeping, constantly on guard and over aware of his surroundings until safely crated and covered. This has been one of the most difficult things to cope with. Even though I bought Jak some great puppy toys, when he played out in the garden with me, his favourite items were, an old gardening glove that he had discovered in a clump of reeds and a wooden scrubbing brush.

I suppose I should have deduced from this that Jak was possessive over things that were ours. Things he had pinched. And maybe I should never have let this trait continue. When Jak was a baby, he was so cute that I just didn't feel the need to be strict over every small issue. But Jak is definitely still an opportunist thief.

Jak has always been very food motivated and any sort of treat or snack constantly trumped toys. Jak also never played on his own either. He lost interest in any toy as soon as I moved away from the game. This is one reason why Jak took up so much of my time in the early months after he came to live with us. I had not ever experienced a dog who cannot play on his own, especially if a new toy is involved. But Jak needed to bump, push, nip and bark constantly when I was in the room wanting me to play with him. I had not had a dog that was so 'clingy' before. Other puppies had been interested in their surroundings and played a lot.

Sometimes I have wondered what life would have been like had I have taken two puppies from the litter. Obviously even just saying that makes me feel like a crazy lady. I have hardly been able to cope with the puppy I got, how could two have possibly been an improvement?

I do wonder though, if Jak would have played differently with another puppy of the same age. Although, on the day when I initially visited the litter, Jak was pootling about on his own.

Later on, too, I wondered whether having a second Collie puppy would ease the situation, perhaps Jak would be focussed on the other dog and not need me to be with him all the time.

I am not convinced that this could have ever been a realistic possibility. We were already living in chaos.

Jak and Jessie

You will remember that we had a very old, and very docile, golden Cocker Spaniel living at home. Jessie had shared her space with Twix for many years, so I imagined that she would adjust easily to the new puppy. Jessie was, after all, partially blind, sometimes deaf and very slow on her feet. Maybe having a new puppy would bring out her playful side? Yet another assumption of mine that proved to be very wrong.

Years ago, Jessie had played incessantly, trying to get Twix (the cute but raggedy windswept looking black and tan Miniature Pinscher type puppy) to play in our big garden in South Africa. Jessie was so playful that she often bowled Twix over, rolling him over the turf as she galloped over him. As Twix grew, he learned to deflect Jessie's playful advances by giving a growl or a sharp snap and playtime was over.

Poor Jessie, I thought, when I knew Twix was leaving. I felt I was doing Jessie a favour by getting a more playful companion for her. When Jak arrived though, Jessie very quickly decided that Jak was a threat to her, to her possessions, to her food and it seemed as if Jessie decided the quicker she killed off the opposition the better.

Jessie waited for opportunities where I wasn't watching and attacked Jak full on time after time. They had to be separated. This was not only very stressful, but also a real pain and definitely something that had not figured in my new puppy plan. It was really difficult keeping the dogs apart even although I tried to keep Jak in a penned off area.

It worked for a few weeks but soon Jak started protesting about his place in a pen and it wasn't long before it became safer for Jak to be crated than hear him constantly bark or throw himself against the mesh of the pen. I was worried that Jak would escape his pen whilst the family were out and Jessie would hurt him badly or even kill him.

Shortly after Jak became part of our family, we had a holiday booked in a small cottage on the harbour at Conwy. Jak and Jessie were totally incompatible and as there was no garden I picked up the job of walking them both independently several times a day.

Jessie whined if she was kept in her travel bed and Jak barked if left in his crate. The holiday was not at all relaxing for me despite this being the first occasion that Jak was let off the lead and he began his recall sessions really well. At this stage I was still feeling that training would solve all our issues. The reality was, however, that our troubles had not yet truly begun.

When we got back home after a full on and stressful week, I searched online and signed Jak up for a series of puppy training classes held in a School Hall locally that promised to produce a well behaved and happy puppy. How I longed for that. Even just one month in I could see that I was battling to keep Jak under any sort of control.

On the very first training session I realised that attending these classes was to be much harder than I had thought. I was told to bring lots of chopped up hot dog sausages as training treats. Jak loved these and was excited to do anything to earn them.

All the puppies in the small hall were to be kept on a lead and we were instructed that the puppies were not to sniff one another. In my mind denying puppies what they desired so much, to explore other puppies and learn how to meet and greet, was a big mistake. The atmosphere was tense and there were several large puppies who were not happy. Several different sized puppies jumped at Jak straining on their leads and growling or snapping and that was Jak done.

I was appalled at what I perceived as learned behaviour! I imagined Jak thinking "I get hot dog treats when I jump and growl at other dogs". This single behaviour trait has been one of the two biggest issues I have continually struggled with. The other is Jak being afraid of meeting strangers, especially men, even though there is no evidence that any man has ever hurt Jak.

Other than those two issues Jak was great....he was quite nippy and bit a lot when he got excited and he did get excited very easily. Just seeing any of our family from a distance or when he heard any sort of noise Jak flew into an excited and noisy episode. I spent much of my time with Jak trying lots of 'calm down' things.

Jak really was the sweetest dog when he was calm or relaxed. But those moments were few and far between. And as Jak grew bigger the calm and relaxed moments diminished until we never saw them at all.

Jessie was still struggling with life which was sad. Of course it was now November and the fireworks going off at night didn't help her. Jak wasn't bothered by the fireworks thanks to the sound therapy and noise desensitization that his breeder had done with the litter. He did sometimes go out and bark at them when he saw the showers of light in the sky. But he was not afraid.

The relationship between Jak and Jessie was tempestuous and changed almost daily over the first ten months of the dogs living under the same roof. Just being in the kitchen with the two dogs was stressful and also unpredictable. Jak was getting taller and he seemed to be learning behaviour from Jessie so he, too, was sometimes looking for a fight.

By January I was beginning to see adolescent behaviour from Jak. He was just six months old. My own personality is one of 'never give up'. So I kept trying new ways to make my increasingly difficult life with the two dogs more tolerable. I tried to train Jessie to go back into her bed with a biscuit after a quick run in the garden in the early morning. Jak was supposed to be learning how to play with his toys by himself without constantly asking me to play.

But Jak really disliked playing by himself, or indeed, doing anything without my constant presence and active input. Later on in the morning it was Jessie's turn to come out and lie in her favourite spot.

At this point Jak was supposed to lie down on the rug under my chair. Jak was constantly unable to manage this unless he was on his lead and having constant corrections.

This strict regime did stop the episodes of fighting indoors for the time being thankfully. The dogs were now able to go out into the garden together in the daylight too. This was a huge relief to me. I really do not do conflict and having it daily in my kitchen was desperate for me.

I remember writing to Katy that I had to be 'Hitler in the Kitchen' at times to keep the peace.

I kept working towards taking Jak to other rooms of the house with me so that Jessie could relax and neither of them needed to be in their crates. But it all seemed too exciting or too worrying for Jak. He could not settle anywhere at all at any time of day.During this period of time I was in the kitchen virtually all day unless the dogs were in their respective crates.

I thought of myself a bit like the traffic directing policeman in Toytown. Standing between the two dogs waving my arms and directing their movements to keep them apart. There were moments where I had both dogs sitting and was able to feed them treats one at a time but those events were rare. I felt very desperate. How I managed to get my full quota of work done I have no idea. There were certainly many days where one or other or both of the dogs were crated more than I would have liked.

Visitors

In the early months of Jak being with us, we invited several dog friendly visitors to the house. It was obvious immediately that Jak was scared of people he did not know. He avoided all strangers even if they had biscuits or treats or attempted to play ball with him. If I picked him up, so that the visitors could see him, he squirmed uncomfortably and if visitors approached he did puppy growls. There was obviously an element of fear from a very young age.

No matter what methods I came up with, Jak could not be persuaded to settle in a room with people he did not know really well. I tried really hard with this because I knew that socialization is so important at an early age.

When my son, Jordon and his wife Kirsten, came to stay with us it took a full twenty-four hours for Jordon to be able to interact properly with Jak. Even though Jordon had never met a dog that did not like him before. In contrast, Jak got on with Kirsten very easily. They were friends immediately.

Not wanting to be beaten Jordon spent a very long time patting the floor and Jak's paws in a playful manner until Jak relaxed enough to be able to play. Then they became friends. I know of no reason for Jak to dislike men. He just always goes into anxiety mode when he meets men, or sees them even at some distance.

Jak also did not like any children who visited the house. He seemed very disturbed if strangers were making a noise in the house and he was very on edge the whole time visitors were in the house. And it took hours for him to calm down after we had had visitors. Days sometimes. When Natasha, my daughter had school friends over to visit Jak always ended up in his crate. Even there, where he should have felt safe, he was barking and growling endlessly. I had not experienced this behaviour before and nothing I researched helped me with this.

Now that Jak is full size I am still working with him on this issue. Mary and Colin, my sister and brother-in-law visit us regularly. The first two evenings that they visited they spent a long time trying to tempt Jak to accept a biscuit from their hands but Jak was very anxious and badly behaved.

One weekend, I travelled with Jak to Mary's house and there Jak was remarkably well behaved. Even allowing Mary to do some training with him. We stayed a few hours and I felt very uplifted by this visit. It felt like the visitor issue could be solved at some point.

But the next time that Mary and Colin visited us at home Jak obviously recognized Mary but was still very badly behaved whenever Colin talked or leaned over to take a scone from the plate. I felt really frustrated and found the situation embarrassing. I have always been an 'open house' sort of person and really dislike that I cannot have visitors to our home.

A few weeks later Mary and Colin visited our house again and I met them at the front door and filled their coat pockets with dog biscuits. Then I just let both them and Jak into the lounge to see what would happen without me trying to manage the situation. I know that underneath all his issues Jak is a lovely and quite soppy dog. I just wish that he could relax and be himself.

Jak smelled the biscuits straight away and he was a different dog. He tried sitting and lying down or any tricks he could think of to get the biscuits from our guests. This was looking so much better. But with this new truce, there also was more chaos. After a few minutes, Jak was launching himself across the lounge and on and off the laps of my visitors. Jak, even at this age, was big and solid. A great lump to arrive suddenly on ones lap, especially after flying through the air.

It was terrible behaviour, and although my guests were polite enough to laugh at the situation, inviting other people to the house was unimaginable. Yet again, I despaired. This was unacceptable behaviour for me but unless Jak was sent to his crate and fastened in, I was unable to control him.

My plan over the coming months and years is to meet up with willing 'guinea pig visitors' who are happy to be barked at and growled at, then jumped all over and inappropriately licked. I am hoping that lots of interaction with people Jak does not know will help him to learn that people are not a threat.

I suppose, over the months, I had recognised some signs of guarding issues in this. Jak was very noisy when he saw the postman, or the bin men or if anyone rang the doorbell. On the days where Jak was most highly strung he even growled at me if I answered the telephone and literally tried to hold me back with his teeth if I went to answer the door bell.

When I researched this, I found that most dogs who displayed guarding behaviour seemed to be over protective or resource guarding. I tried all the recommended training tips I found but Jak's behavior, in this regard, did not change at all.

This was, and still is, a complex problem. Some days Jak can behave better with these issues and some days it seems impossible to get through to him whatsoever.

Jak meets Mizzle

It was December time when Jak finally got to visit Katy and Mizzle. I was very worried about the meeting. Would Mizzle attack Jak on her home turf? Would Jak wee all over Katy's house and bark and bite?

Jak was still small and had his cute fuzzy puppy fur. He looked adorable....until you got up close! Katy and I had emailed each other lots before the visit trying to anticipate anything that could go wrong. Neither of us could possibly have imagined how 'full on' the weekend would be and in particular the Grandma incident that was to occur.

Before we turned up at Katy's door, I had warned Katy about Jak and his current behaviour. I explained that I had a naughty Jak and I had a super lovely loving Jak. I had no idea which dog he would be on the day! It always seemed to be one or the other. No in between. I knew that Jak would be a very excitable dog, whichever mood he was in.

Jak's big teeth were coming through and he was doing a lot of chewing on hands and shoes whenever he got the chance. More than usual although Jak had always been a very mouthy puppy. I was worried that people would think Jak was always a horrible biting dog!

This was an ongoing worry for me. I knew that deep down Jak was a lovely soppy dog, but his true character, was hardly ever seen. And with strangers there was no chance.

When Jak was fully grown I was able to share videos and clips of his clever tricks but strangers were just not able to meet him. From about nine in the evenings Jak was a lovely sleepy boy, however, the rest of the time he was constantly looking for something to do. His solution was usually finding noisy barking things or naughty ripping or chewing things to do.

In any case Jak never lay down and dozed. He was completely full on and needed constant supervision to keep him, and everything else, safe.

When I planned to visit Katy I took Jak's bedtime crate and I also had a crate in the car so that there were places to put Jak if he was out of control. Katy was convinced that, after having the two very long walks a day that Mizzle enjoys, Jak would be tired and calm. I doubted it. I guessed that Mizzle would be needing a break from Jak after a long walk with him!

Mizzle had always looked like the perfect companion and family dog to me. Serene and well behaved. Katy felt that Mizzle would tell Jak when she had had enough pestering without the on-going fighting that I had witnessed with Jessie and Jak. Again, I was not so sure and so, I was rather anxious about their meeting.

Katy planned for lots of outdoor play for the dogs together as well as the long farmland walks. Katy was really looking forward to meeting Jak properly and us spending time with both dogs together. When Jak first arrived at Katy's house he went into the garden with Mizzle who seemed only marginally interested.

As Jak got to see that Mizzle would play and not attack he relaxed just a bit and began to play. Of course, in true Jak style, he then went completely crazy and did not stop running, jumping, nipping and generally causing noisy chaos.

A move into the lounge resulted in Jak leaping onto the back of the cream leather corner sofa and running the entire length of it. As he ran at top speed, leaping and barking, he displaced sofa seated occupants one by one. Jak was followed by me chasing after in an ineffectual, and most embarrassing, attempt to recapture the beast.

I was stressed, breathless, and absolutely mortified at Jak's behavior. I remembered how when my children were young I taught them how to behave calmly and quietly in other people's houses. It was something that was important for me and I felt completely at a loss as to how to teach Jak to be calm and possibly respectable.

I had my recurring feeling that this puppy nightmare would only end if I took Jak away and we lived together on a remote mountain where there were no people. Which, to be fair, I probably wouldn't mind trying, although money would be an issue. At this point of Jak's relationship with our family and extended family I think everyone would have let out a sigh of relief if the chaos had stopped.

Between Katy, Mizzle and myself we managed to calm Jak down and replace his lead. I tried to keep him calm, but it was always just out of my grasp. By the time afternoon came we had taken both dogs out for a really long run. Jak was lying at my feet and he was actually half asleep. This was better behaviour. Long may it last.

Katy had previously warned me that Grandma was coming for tea. "Don't let Jak pester Grandma" she warned. Grandma was getting on in years and did not like dogs at all.

"It will be okay. We will know when Grandma is arriving" she assured me. So I was sitting on the floor in front of the warm log burner, Jak at my side his lead held gently in my hand. I was so relaxed, sleepy myself almost.....when suddenly the door opened and Grandma's cheery "Hello" rang out.

In a billionth of a second Jak had leapt up, run the length of the lounge and leapt up on Grandma high enough to plant a slobbery kiss on her cheek, he then proceeded to bark at Grandma whilst cleverly evading all hands that were trying to restrain him.

I am sure that the moment only lasted for perhaps a minute but to me, time travelled so slowly that it seemed to take forever before Jak was restrained and put in his crate whilst we brushed Grandma down and tried to resume normal service.

I was quite shaken up. It is a feeling I often have with Jak if I am unable to get any sort of control over him. Although Jak is now approaching eighteen months old, there are still hours and indeed, whole days, where I am unable to communicate to him because of his over anxious, over aroused and over excited attitude.

Today I have learned that the more excited Jak gets, the less capable he is of listening or remembering how he should act. On internet chat rooms and dog training pages owners refer to this as the dog 'having a full bucket'. It has taken me a long time to appreciate that Jak's bucket is obviously very small. It fills very quickly and when Jak has been over stimulated it takes a disproportionate length of time for him to calm down to being relaxed again.

In fact, if Jak has been over excited or anxious for several hours, it really may take days for him to come back down to calm behaviour. This is very inconvenient indeed. But I have got to know that being patient and waiting it out is definitely a more productive plan than trying to force calm behaviour.

Mizzle was very good with Jak over the weekend, and every subsequent visit we made. Playing with him in the garden and telling him with a brief snap when enough was enough. But if we had not had the crate available in the other room every visit to Katy's would have been impossible. Where once Katy and I used to spend hours chatting about life and laughing together, now just keeping Jak in control took all of my time unless Jak was in his crate.

To Jak's credit, he did sleep well at night in the crate. And he always has. I would never have coped with the days if the nights had been unsettled too. Perhaps it would have been better to take notes of all the good things Jak did achieve rather than to keep re-playing the bad moments! It would certainly have been better for my mental health.

First Training Camp for Jak

When it became apparent that Jak was unruly, and that I was struggling with his behaviour at an early age, I had looked into options for training him. Because the puppy classes had been such a disaster I discounted similar venues straight away. I came across a residential dog training company on the internet that offered training on site and after chatting to them on the telephone what they had to offer seemed really good. I was hopeful that in the hands of more experienced dog trainers than me some progress may be made.

Our family was going away in the February half term and the dogs would be going to our local kennels anyway so this seemed like the ideal opportunity. In fact, it was perfect timing because Jessie and Jak could not be kennelled together like Twix and Jessie used to be.

February half term came around and I was so ready for a break from Jak and also very hopeful that things would turn around. The training kennels were excellent. Jak stayed with them for the full ten days and they worked hard with him each day. When I went to pick Jak up I had the opportunity to do some supervised training with Jak for an hour. We did lots of lead walking in the training yard. Jak had learned how to walk to heel properly when asked. He was looking for instruction from me and walked like a beautiful and well trained dog.

However, his trainer shared with me that there had been issues. Jak was extremely anxious with people he didn't know, especially men, and with other dogs until he got to know them. Especially other dogs who were on leads.

This was a real blow. Jak's trainer felt that Jak was lacking in confidence and that this was a big problem for him. She assured me that Jak had gained a bit more confidence in the time he had been in training.

Meanwhile, I had been reading books by Cesar Milan and had decided to try working with Jak and Jessie as a pack rather than keep trying to have them living semi separate.

So I tried more play times for them together with me policing the events. I tried feeding them both at the same time too. For a while it seemed to be working. But Jessie's obsession with food and chews were problematic. On the 4th March despite a couple of months of relative peace time Jessie started the scrapping again. Jessie had caused the fight by sneaking into Jak's bed and taking one of his plastic bones into her bed. When Jak sniffed around her bed, obviously aware his bone was there, Jessie started a fight.

I noticed that straight away Jak became more nervous again. Was it Jessie's initial behaviour that had caused Jak's lack of confidence that the training kennels worked with?

Anyway, in case you are feeling really sad for Jak, don't be too hasty because since he arrived home with more confidence, he had been hounding Jessie to play whenever he was with her and there had already been a couple of (well deserved) warning snaps.

Jak was very quick to learn what things to do to get Jessie's attention. He would nip at her ears as she walked by him, or push her off track as she headed to her bed. As Jessie could not see or hear well, she would repeatedly jump in surprise. Then one day Jessie had a real go at Jak again. This time whilst they were sitting waiting for their food.

I suppose food being very important to Jessie made her more inclined to attack when they were being fed at the same time. The fighting was more prolonged but, thankfully, even though it had sounded vicious, when the noise and excitement had abated neither dog was injured.

Jessie had to be kept in her bed more for her safety after this. Now that Jak was much bigger and no longer backing down to Jessie the fights went on for longer and the dogs were harder to break up.

This left me with the situation that neither Jak nor Jessie were getting the exercise they needed. Jessie was currently being cooped up more each day in order to allow Jak to be out of his crate.

So, in any case, Hitler in the kitchen was no longer working. A new plan had to be found. Jak and Jessie were not happy together, although it seemed to be rather a case of Jessie not being happy and Jak being very confused.

From this point on I regularly considered whether it would be best to rehome Jak. As much as I loved him, and I did truly believe that his natural temperament was friendly, despite the behaviour I had seen. But life with Jak was exceedingly trying every single day. It could never be an option to rehome Jessie in her elderly, incapacitated state.

My worry with rehoming Jak was that, because he looked so beautiful, lots of people would want to choose him from the rehoming kennels. But, surely, after a few days of his unpredictable and uncontrollable attitude he would be back there time and time again. I thought about what this would do to Jak's anxious state and his mistrust of people and I just cried. I could not let our journey end like this. I would never forgive myself.

I started sitting in the kitchen to watch television every evening with Jak on his lead. I am not a television watcher by nature, but I was really struggling to survive evenings. I was tired and mentally exhausted and Jak was at his very worst just before bedtime. I did not want either dog to have to stay in their crate all evening, but they just had to be kept apart.

Jak needed to be with me, but this required constant challenging over his behaviour, even on the lead. There was one memorable evening when I fell asleep in my chair in front of the tiny wall mounted television. Jak was tied to my chair leg with his long lead. He was quietly chewing the biggest chew you have ever seen when I nodded off. Several minutes later, Jak jumped on top of me whacking me several times around the face with the chew. It was not exactly bad behaviour and I suppose it would have been quite funny had I not received painful injuries to my jaw and lips.

As this story of Jak and Jessie evolved, Jak became bigger, and bigger until he was at least twice Jessie's size and very strong.

The fighting issue had turned around and I became worried that Jessie would be the one to be hurt or killed. If Jessie started a fight Jak retaliated very strongly and separating the two snarling, snapping dogs was becoming very difficult. Shouting and jumping up and down or even throwing water no longer shocked the dogs into parting so that one of them could be moved away.

Home was a very stressful place to be for all of us. I had to admit that my leadership skills and attitude needed to change to keep both dogs safe.

Starting Walking

I could not wait to get out and walk Jak on his lead when he first arrived. Many years ago I had had a dog that I took for long walks daily. Easily six miles plus walking with Pasha on the lead to clear my head, organise my thoughts and tire my mind and body.

At first I was sure that Jak was going to love this. I bought a brown wax jacket and fur-lined walking wellies so that we could walk every day despite the weather and I was so excited.

Jak arrived at our home in early October but already by early December I was stressed by the issues we struggled with when I walked with Jak. By Christmas my wax jacket was torn ragged and smelt strongly of fish due to the dried fish that I used as rewards for recall. When Jak had eaten his fish and was back on the lead he constantly mouthed my right arm sometimes nipping through the fabric and pinching my skin. I seemed to be covered in bruises all the time.

I was at a loss to know what to do. Jak did not respond to verbal commands such as 'No' or 'Leave' at all. He just seemed to zone them out and carry on misbehaving. When he was still tiny I would pick him up and tuck him under my arm when his behaviour got badly out of line. He was growing quickly though and soon I could not safely carry him.

I was convinced that this bad behaviour was over excitement or over tiredness as it always happened after some running around. It did not occur to me at this time that Jak's issue could be over stimulation or even anxiety at being outside.

At first I used to take a small throwing toy with me on walks. Jak loved playing. Unfortunately I found that Jak's excitement levels grew so quickly when playing with a toy that he would get snappy and would nip and bite hard. Obviously, I was always the target.

Each day when I put the toy away at the end of a walk Jak erupted into an angry attack mode. It only took a matter of weeks before all my clothes were shabby and had jagged bite marks on them. Within a matter of weeks the new wax jacket had ripped pockets and a shredded right sleeve from where Jak had jumped up constantly to demand his toy. My jeans, too were very torn, and not in a fashionable way. My legs and arms were covered with painful bruises from the constant nipping. Walking had become a contact sport. I very quickly stopped wearing any clothes that I cared about any day, and I always dressed in old clothes instead.

So, I discovered that just a couple of months into Jak ownership I was walking around wearing old muddy and ripped clothes, I smelled like a fishwife because of Jak's fishy treats and I was bruised, battered and almost defeated. In truth I looked a whole lot worse than that description reads.

My confidence levels plummeted. I could not do this. I was not able to cope with this daily onslaught. Jak had really taken over my life, and not in a good way. I was constantly revamping my routines and finding new training methods to try to keep on top of the new issues that seemed to emerge daily.

It was certainly a fact that as soon as I headed off one bad habit a new one cropped up. It was a continuous challenge and I was very, very tired. I had read up a huge amount about lead training and was hoping that exercise would cause tiredness which would result in Jak sleeping and in turn this would bring calmness.

Katy often reminded me how much exercise Collies needed and I tried my best to find ways in which to be able to manage Jak on walks but it was getting harder and harder.

Some of my earliest worries came from walking Jak from our house and into the cul-de-sac where we lived. Jak walked well at first on a loose puppy lead and listened to me when I asked him to 'heel'. But just a couple of days into walking outside the house and garden Jak started to show great anxiety towards noises, cars and any activity in the estate we lived on.

Jak was great off the lead and also on a long training rope but only for a really short time. If the walk lasted longer than about fifteen minutes Jak became uncontrollable and was most definitely no longer listening to me.

I quickly had to ban any toy throwing or running/chasing on walks because of Jak's over excitement and his painful nipping and biting. Jak really acted like a police dog taking down a runaway robber grabbing my arms or legs and leaving those huge rips in my clothes. All of this occurred before Jak was four months in age.

Day by day Jak's anxiety grew and he started barking and growling at unknown dangers. My anxiety started to grow too. I would hear a dog barking way in the distance and look to Jak knowing that he would react. (Later in this book you will find how I managed to combat this if this is an issue that you and your dog also struggle with). Walks quickly became unpleasant and scary. Certainly not a time that I looked forward to.

As Jak's reactions grew my fear of taking him out on the lead also grew. Because of Jak's love of food, titbits and treats, walking off the lead was an easier option if I could find a dog, people and traffic free space. Jak was very quickly trained to five short blasts on a gundog whistle and so long as a treat was forthcoming Jak zoomed to my side every single time the whistle sounded and very promptly too. I always carried the small dried fish in my pocket to reward Jak with for the really quick recalls.

Even getting in a daily ten minute 'off the lead' run had become difficult though. There was a place that I found where I could park the car and walk up a big hill. This was fine so long as firstly, there was a car parking space and secondly, there were no other people or dogs walking there. Some days I drove up two or three times just to come back again with no walking.

I just could not find a safe place to exercise Jak and I felt that this lack of exercise was not helping him to relax at home.

After Christmas, I decided that I must persevere with Jak and his difficult walking.

It was not the case that Jak did not want to walk to heel, he was very attentive to that if I had treats with me. It was more the fact that Jak got anxious whenever he heard a noise or saw a person.

If he saw a dog he lunged growling and snarling like a really vicious dog. Nothing seemed to be stopping this and Jak was getting bigger and stronger every day. Some days I could barely hold him back without getting almost pulled over.

People I spoke to about this felt that I was not firm enough with Jak and that I must try to become a better 'Leader' in order that he would obey me. This sounded like good logic and, at the time, I constantly blamed myself for Jak's behaviour. But it was really hard to exude confidence and leadership when so much daily chaos was going on.

After just a few weeks of me trying to implement any type of lead training or reactive dog training I had run out of places to walk. Both Jak and I were anticipating problems before we even left the house. Worse still Jak was getting into an anxious body stance as soon as we got out of the door or even as soon as he saw the lead!

So I was really finding that getting Jak enough exercise was a struggle. Not because I didn't have the time or the energy but because I was working so hard on trying to get him to ignore people, dogs and traffic. It was very tiring for both of u. Sometimes, the strategies I read about or researched on the internet worked for a few days each time I tried a new approach. But nothing seemed to be working long term.

Jak was definitely approaching adolescence and testing all the boundaries daily. I tried hard to get him to be less reactive with seeing people when we walked but it was noisy and hard work. People did not have to be close to us in order for Jak to react. Every person set him off into an anxious display. Even sometimes people that he had previously met and been alright with.

I found a new walk in some woods nearby that was quieter. We had not seen any dog walkers there, but we had to walk from the car which was parked in a noisy and busy industrial estate.

Each day that I took Jak on this new walk, he became more and more nervous as I opened the car boot to get him out of the car. As we walked past the industrial units and lorry distribution centres, there was a lot of noise from machinery in the units. We soon got to the stage that Jak was already wound as tight as a spring even before I put his lead on in the boot of the car. I later found out that these woods were well documented online as a place where men could go to pick up men. Much as that was quite funny and probably explained the lack of dog walkers, it was no longer a place where we could walk because of Jak's anxious reaction to the noise.

Then one evening, right outside our own front door, something really happened. I went to take Jak out for a short lead walk around our local streets. Just in our own small cul de sac we saw six dogs and eleven cars in the space of about five minutes. I could not believe that so many people mill about so much.

There were also neighbours chatting on doorsteps and ringing each other's doorbells. Jak just totally lost the plot and I had a long and embarrassing struggle to get him back home. Once there I consigned Jak to his crate and just cried.

Things were going from difficult, to bad, to impossible. I was truly at my wits end. I decided that perhaps even more exercise would be the best plan. I tried to be prepared for lots of distractions and manage them as best as I could each walk. It wasn't easy though, or fun, and walking Jak became a real chore instead of a joy. I was miserable and very unsure of how things would turn out. I looked carefully at the places I was walking and tried to minimise contact with other people or dogs which was really difficult.

I varied having Jak on the lead, or running free when I was in a quiet place, and continually practiced his recall which he did very well. It was very rare though to have one whole walk that went without incident.

To make matters worse, some dog owners were very abusive to me, shouting loudly and very rudely. One man who was actually reading a newspaper and not watching his big dog at all was the worst culprit. His dog was on an extending lead and yet this man blamed me when his dog ran over to Jak. I was trying to keep a distance between the two dogs but the other dog had a lot of play in his extending lead. Jak lunged at the dog all teeth and snarls, looking very vicious. "That dog needs putting down," the man shouted. I was horribly upset and didn't sleep for many nights worrying about the future.

Although I tried every combination of places to walk and different approaches of walking with lead on or lead off, nothing was really close to solving these walking issues. Jak was nervous walking in new places. But also, if an incident took place somewhere, on any return visit to that place Jak was ready for a fight before we had even met anyone.

I was so upset because I really wanted to be able to enjoy walking Jak. I wanted him to get the daily exercise he needed and I really didn't want to struggle for years with these issues.

A dog is for life was beginning to sound like a life sentence.

Minor Improvements

I started driving to a nearby field and just walking with Jak off the lead throwing a gundog dummy for exercise. If there was already a person in the field I drove by and tried again later. It became very stressful as well as time consuming. When another dog walker appeared whilst we were already in the field I called Jak and put his lead on. But on the lead Jak jumped up and bit my hand and arm hard over and over again. Even just walking from the car to the gate of the field became difficult. I now hated dog walking time.

By this time I had decided to abandon the walking through the woods near the industrial estate totally as we had had two bad experiences. Also as soon as we arrived at the start of the path Jak was creating a major fuss without even seeing people or dogs. We were then both too tense to walk at all. Exercise for both of us was getting less and less.

Jak was still unable to walk past dogs without reacting, but I was having quite a lot of success with him sitting, on the lead, and watching other dogs walking from a short distance. In fact, the only noises he made were excited 'I want to play' noises. I was to learn later that Jak loved playing with other dogs if they were all off the lead. In fact Jak didn't even mind being on the lead himself if the other dogs were loose. If they ran up to him he behaved in a proper way. Meeting and greeting correctly. It was so strange that his fear came when other dogs were on leads.

Meanwhile, I had read a lot of advice online about anxious dogs needing plenty of time to relax after an incident. Looking at Jak this way, I could see that he was often badly shaken and unable to calm down after even the most minor incident. From this time, when Jak got over anxious or when there had been an incident, I stopped walks for a day or so in an effort to allow him to try to calm down fully again.

This did leave me with his excess energy to deal with. We did lots of training in the kitchen and lots of playing in the garden but, obviously, Jak has enough energy to run up and down mountains all day so it was impossible to release all that latent energy. This, in turn, led to more bad behaviour around the house. Obsessive running between the kitchen door and the back door, barking, running along the kitchen worktops, jumping on the dining table and even on top of the upright piano. Jak was limited only by his imagination when exercising himself.

For the rest of the family this was a chaotic time. We stopped eating together at the dining table as meals could not be peaceful or without interruption. Attention seeking was Jak's middle name and he tried more and more until he had sent the rest of the family out of the room and had me to himself. We could all see what he was doing but it seemed impossible to stop.

I tried taking Jak to the hill where he could run free very early in the mornings. Just like when Jak was smaller I noticed that walks excited and stressed him so much that he was unable to relax or calm down at all at home! So I started only walking in the afternoons.

This made a huge difference. When Jak came out of his crate in the mornings he was always sleepy and cuddly wanting fuss and company. I discovered that spending calm time with him in the mornings was much better than trying to go out for stressful walks.

Other than the walking stresses Jak was becoming a beautiful and lovely dog. I was feeling more positive, hoping that there would now be a slow but steady improvement.

Since coming back from the training kennels Jak had continued to wear a cord slip collar that the kennels had trained him with and provided. It stayed loose when Jak walked nicely, but if he pulled or lunged it tightened up.

The cord was quite long though, and so, I had to pull my hands up high to take up the slack and jerk as required. This became awkward and as Jak was growing taller my short stature began to be a new problem.

I had also noticed that Jak seemed to be starting to work out exactly how much he could pull or lunge without strangling himself. But sometimes, if the dog he wanted to lunge at was really close, he went further and as the cord became seriously uncomfortable around his neck he lashed out with redirected anger biting my leg or any part of me that was near him.

My instinct has always been to put my left leg against Jak to try to push him away from whoever he was lunging at. Soon all of my walking jeans were badly ripped and I had a battered and bruised leg above the knee. Worse still, I had a deep two pronged bite in my thigh that was so deep it would not heal.

This injury occurred one day when walking Jak on the lead in a huge countryside park where I could see for miles. I could generally change my route to avoid other walkers here and we tended to be quite relaxed while Jak was on the lead.

Suddenly a big black dog ran up to us from nowhere and started to growl and snap at Jak. I could not see anyone around at all so I shouted loudly to announce there was a problem. Jak and the dog were full on scrapping around my legs and there was nothing I could do. Eventually the owner appeared and called off her dog.

Jak was still over excited and aggressive and still on the lead, and so, he bit me deeply on my thigh, stopping as I cried out. Jak became instantly submissive, licking my hands and legs. We got home but I was desperately worried. I had done all I could in that situation and, because of another dog and owner, blood had been spilled. Fortunately, that blood was mine.

I still had decisions to make regarding how to approach walking Jak and I turned to Katy for more advice. These were the options I could see and had to choose from:

1/ To keep trying to have Jak watch, or interact, with dogs whilst on the lead using two new techniques: a Halti collar to try and stop him lunging and snarling, or by tapping him on the nose with the end of the lead when he thought about putting his angry dog act on. This would probably mean that Jak would continue to try to get feisty and I would continue to get stressed out.

2/ To organise a training session with Jak's trainer from the residential kennels in a park local to the kennels. The trainer had offered to have a session there where there were other people and dogs to see if she could help me with the issues.

3/ To try to walk Jak off the lead where I knew there were dogs and people and be brave enough to put up with other people being cross with me if he ran up and wouldn't come away. Obviously my control over Jak was minimal, but I didn't think he would be so feisty off the lead. This option felt very risky though, as I knew I was not in full control of Jak and his behaviour. What if he were to turn really vicious?

4/ To just do nothing. Continue to walk Jak in our normal field daily, even though he would not always get enough exercise (for example if other people or dogs were there). Wait until Jak turned 12 months old (August) then have him neutered. Give Jak more calming down time and then try doing more exercise again.

At the time I felt that option four was the easiest and the path of least resistance. I was tempted to try option three as it would give Jak a variation on walking venues but I felt that Jak liked the predictability of the one field. And I was aware of how upset I got when people shouted at me for not having Jak under full control.
If it went well it would be great for us both but if it went badly it would be another real set back.

Jak was able to walk beautifully to heel on the choke collar (cord not chain) that was supplied from the training kennels when there were no distractions. But when Jak saw a person or a dog he went into full lunging snarling mode and just almost strangled himself as there was no stopper on the collar. I was worried that as I couldn't control him until the distraction had gone he might actually choke himself as in the moment he was getting beside himself and quite obviously not thinking clearly at all.

It became very clear to me that all this was to do with his fear of unknown dogs even though his time at the training kennels proved that he was friendly with other dogs when he met them properly. And subsequent meetings with dogs where Jak could play had been great too.

Katy recommended that I try to get much more exercise for Jak. She felt that he needed to be in a calm state before being introduced to the things that wind him up when he was on the lead. Katy also wondered if Jak was protecting me or feeling trapped because he was on the lead. We both felt that more professional input was required.

I wondered whether I could get Jak some exercise in a different manner so I looked online for suggestions. I did think about trying crazy exercise options like rollerblading with Jak or Bike Joring where the dog wears a harness and pulls a bike or scooter like a husky pulls a sledge. I knew, though, that these pulling options required Jak to be 12 months old even to train for them. I decided that when Jak was old enough I would definitely pursue these activities. They looked so much fun online.

For my life at this time I felt that Jak on the lead, and the ongoing Jessie and Jak saga were the two biggest stresses I had.

I realize that compared to many people's lives my issues could seem quite minor but I found the conflict day after day so upsetting.

Books and internet searching did not help as everywhere I read that once these things started they were almost impossible to stop. I hated that I could not fix these issues.

I was also aware that Jak wasn't getting the exercise he needed but the options seemed so limited. I decided that it was better for Jak to avoid bad experiences rather than to keep having them daily thus reinforcing his view of people and dogs as a threat.

I also felt that so much more could be achieved if I wasn't so scared of getting into situations I couldn't cope with. Or if I could ignore the rude dog walkers who shouted at me!

The trouble was that to a certain extent I agreed with them. Jak needed to be under better control.

A Prisoner in the Kitchen

On reading the title of this chapter you may be thinking that poor Jak has been kept, a prisoner, against his will in a kitchen whilst we, his family were living it up somewhere. Far from it, in reality it is I, Jak's beleaguered owner, who has at the writing of this page, been a prisoner in the kitchen for over sixty seven weeks (excluding the weeks Jak was in kennels or away training).

That is a total of more than four hundred and seventy two days and potentially almost six thousand hours of being trapped in the back room of my house. Of course I am exaggerating somewhat. After all when I was out at work I was out of the kitchen (oh the freedom!). Those moments when I ran upstairs to take a speedy shower I escaped the confines of my prison for almost twenty minutes at a time. I can feel a hedonistic rush envelope me just thinking about it.

It is not that the kitchen of my house is an unpleasant environment at all. On the contrary the kitchen is a large room with the added bonus of a small conservatory with patio doors. I have the luxury of a dab radio quietly playing Christian music in the background. There is a cupboard that is, at times, fully stocked with every cereal eaters' best fantasies, although for some reason over the last fifteen months the cereal cupboard often looks sadly depleted or there happens to be an unhappy shortage of fridge-cold milk.

The reason for my imprisonment is, of course, Jak. I am sure you guessed. Jak's behaviour in the kitchen has, over the months since his arrival, been abominable. But his behaviour outside of the kitchen has been at least twenty times worse. Short experiments in the lounge have always ended in shouts, nips, bites, furniture crisis moments, barking and tears...mostly mine. Well the tears anyway.

Short forays into the office, which is mostly the domain of a cat, Smokey the Unpredictable, have always quite expectedly ended in chaos or worse.

When Jak was living in a barn with his siblings the puppies often played with the cats and kittens that lived in the barn. When I say played, I do not mean chased, nipped or tormented. The puppies, including Jak, played very nicely cosying up to the cats, licking them and generally following them around. It was a great thing to see. It made me feel that Jak would love Smokey our resident cat and that would definitely be one less thing to worry about.

And, yes, you guessed it, I was wrong on this occasion as well. When baby Jak discovered that there was a cat in the house he immediately began a campaign of 'must jump all over this cat at any cost'. This campaign included suddenly attacking windows, doors, curtains and venetian blinds, piano mountaineering and standing on the dining table and the sideboard at regular intervals to look out for the feline prey.

Now Smokey is not your typical British, love to sit, placid and purring creature. Smokey, together with Twix and Jessie, arrived at Heathrow Airport one Tuesday very early in the morning, having flown from Eastern Cape South Africa. The pets were exactly a week late and the previous week my husband and son had hired a van and driven to Heathrow very early in the morning. Only to find our pets had not arrived there and so they came home with a Christmas tree in the van, but that is a totally different story!

Smokey was given to my husband as a tiny eight week old kitten. She is a seal-point coloured and long haired, most beautiful looking cat. Unfortunately, I am not a 'cat' person, I am currently beginning to wonder if I am even a 'dog' person! So not being attracted to or attractive to cats I have had several love/hate relationships with cats and kittens. Smokey is no different. Although she looks beautiful and lovely when her owner is around as soon as my husband leaves the room there are sudden attacks or moments of full on despising stares all directed at me.

At night-time when I potter barefoot to the bathroom there are often sudden and painful foot, and especially, toe attacks from under the bed. There could be an unexpected launch from a window sill and all the family remembers the day when Smokey dived out of the open washing machine and bit and clawed my leg as I walked by.

If it were not for the fact that I am aware that washing machines are dangerous places for cats I may have retaliated.

To get back to the story of Jak and Smokey you would think that a mainly outdoor living African wildcat would be more than a match for a tiny Collie puppy. But, because Smokey chose to run away every time she saw Jak, and because Jak thought this was a great game, even the sound of the cat sneaking out of the cat flap became the signal for a chaotic episode. Excited barking, a puppy flying through the air and connecting with the glass panelled kitchen door violently and repeatedly.

Unfortunately, on days where the wind was anything more than a light breeze the cat flap continuously opened and shut with no cat in sight at all. This, of course, wound Jak up more and more until, yet again, the crate was the only place where he could become calm.

But much worse than these incidents were the times when Jak let himself out of the kitchen by depressing the handle lever with his paw and simultaneously pushing the door with his other paw. He would then run hell for leather through the office, up the stairs and play either 'trash the bedrooms' or a very vigorous game of 'hunt the cat' in the main bedroom.

One time Jak even managed to let himself out of the kitchen and ran away, knocking over the rubbish bin which then wedged against the door and totally blocked me from reopening the door.

Honestly, it comes to something when you are in your mid-fifties, have a university level education and consider yourself to be a clever person and yet you are locked in your own kitchen against your will by a six month old UNPEDIGREE Collie!

Frequently I fastened Jak to my waist with a long leather double ended lead. This meant that I knew where he was and what he was up to and I could still prepare food and cook. Although it was certainly not ideal when getting hot things out of the oven. Jak could have stuck his nose in the oven, he could have bodged me and I could have burnt my hands or arms or of course he could have taken off suddenly at great speed whilst I was carrying dinner and a terrible accident could have happened.

At a time of desperation to get Jak thinking more, and maybe to work towards him pulling me on roller skates for exercise, I sometimes cooked dinner wearing my roller skates with Jak fastened to me. It actually went remarkably well, but I had to stop after a few days of doing this as my family members became very stressed as spectators because it all looked so dangerous!

Jak still has to wander around fastened to my waist in the house some of the time because of his terrible behaviour. He is not good at picking up adult dog (or human) 'leave me alone' signals because of his general over excitement at life.

One sign that became imminently important in trying to cope with the behaviour of Jak was the daily position of his ears and of his tail. Each morning when I opened Jak's crate to reveal him eagerly waiting I was a bit scared of what I would see. Some mornings inside the crate was a super fuzzy yawning and stretching cutie pie. On other occasions there was a creature residing in there that would scare any fearless jungle explorer. I knew exactly what my day would hold within two seconds of opening the crate.

I thought that Jak looked forward to me arriving at his crate early in the morning because loved me and wanted a cwtch (a Welsh hug as taught to me by his breeder). Although it is entirely possible, looking back, that it probably was the thought of another chaotic fun filled running round the walls bark fest that Jak was looking forward to each morning.

He certainly got the cwtch over and done with as speedily as possible and got on with his day his way.

Katy had suggested that sometimes Collies can misinterpret what their job in life is and as they are sure that they *should* be working they find their own job. This made a lot of sense and I often pondered what exactly Jak thought his life was all about? Perhaps Jak was under the impression that I had chosen him to reduce the cat to a running white streak. Or to turn the house into an untidy unkempt bombshell area strewn with the sad remains of many items?

There always seemed to be an accumulation of dog toys in various state of deconstruction as well as other peoples' belongings that had left other rooms and never made it home, littering the floor. Perhaps Jak thought that his role was to keep me busy in the kitchen or to make sure that Jessie stayed in her half of the kitchen.

Whatever Jak was thinking his job was at age six months I can confirm now that although he has tried out many canine roles since then, at one year of age it still has not occurred to Jak to work at becoming a happy relaxed and calm family dog!

Jak the Sheepdog?

One of my worries about Jak often would be, what if he should really be a sheepdog? What if Jak had the genetic sheepdog herding instincts and really needed to do this? I read as many books on sheepdogs as possible and spent a lot of time online too and finally decided that before Jak was too old he should try out herding sheep.

If Jak really needed to be a sheepdog then I wasn't above volunteering on a sheep farm and doing further training with him. I was amazed to find out that you can book for lessons and go and learn how to herd sheep with your dog!

My first attempt to discover Jak's shepherding capabilities was when he was just around fourteen weeks old. In November Jak and I attended a sheepdog handling beginner day in with Mainline Border Collie Centre in Yorkshire. There was a lot of learning for me and a lot of waiting in the car for Jak.

I loved working with the dogs in the pen with a few sheep and also in the field moving sheep. It was a real breath of fresh air to me. At the end of the day Jak got his turn. He looked quite worried in the barn with four loose sheep but when the trainer put up a small round pen I was able to work the sheep in the pen and Jak ran around the outside of the pen. So it was all good. I had discovered that Jak did have some potential to learn how to herd sheep although, it must be said, he didn't act as though he dreamed about nothing else!

So training wise, I learnt from Vicki, the trainer, that all I needed to achieve was for Jak to get a solid Lie Down at a distance and a responsive Recall and we would be ready to go and do further training when Jak reached about a year old!

In January I took Jak back to Mainline sheepdog training, this time for one to one general puppy training with Vicki. I had booked a 'Thinking like Canines' one to one training session as Jak was being such a trial, both in the house and on the lead.

It really did appear that at the bottom of all the difficulties with Jak was the problem that although Jak loved me lots and wanted to spend time with me he did not see me as his leader and would not do anything I asked (other than for food). I was already worried that my lack of confidence could be an issue provoking this bad behaviour. If I were the sort of person that commanded a presence when entering a room would Jak possibly take more notice?

As it was Jak would stay lying down whilst I was standing up but as soon as I sat down he ran off. This had been happening forever and had been compounded by the fact that I was getting no rest or relaxation unless Jak was in his crate. At this point on the lead and off the lead in the field Jak was mostly good but if he got over excited he was still biting and nipping me constantly. I could not get him to listen to me at all.

I was hoping that after this training I would be able to control Jak better and because Vicki was also a sheepdog trainer there should be no training that would curb sheepdog training at a later date if that became a firm plan. I had read that if you accidentally train your Collie in a way that affects their relationship with sheep or their confidence they may never be able to herd sheep.

After the session of training, Vicki was of the opinion that although Jak was a lovely dog and had learned well what I had taught him, he was really being an obnoxious teenager. Vicki taught me to talk to Jak as, although he could not understand the words, he would understand the body posture and tone when I was angry or when I was pleased.

This advice was one of the best bits of training I was ever given. It certainly transformed my relationship with Jak. Please don't think that this means we had any of our issues solved or that I had been liberated from the kitchen as yet!

Vicki also told me that Jak had learned to press all of the right buttons to get my attention and his own way although he really knew what he should be doing. In addition, Vicki suggested putting Jak on a short detox diet to clear his system of excess protein which can make dogs, particularly Collies, more hyperactive than necessary.

So when I arrived home Jak went on a two week diet of porridge oats which he loved. He was also on a strict routine at home to try to wait it out until it became his choice to behave calmly. Regarding outdoor walking it was recommended that Jak should walk and exercise on the five metre lead in the field daily and no toys on walks to reduce that excitement.

Jak ate his porridge well. He stopped pestering for food and being so reactive when food was around. And he was definitely less busy. Vicki had said that Jak's world was currently too big and too exciting at present so I should make his world smaller and more controlled until he began to cope with things more calmly. Then I could start expanding his world slowly.

Later Katy confirmed to me that Mizzle had been kept firstly in a crate in the kitchen, then allowed in the kitchen and garden. She was only allowed to go into the lounge after her teenage spell. I, personally, cannot remember Mizzle being anything like naughty or uncontrolled but I suppose it is different if it is your own home.

I am not sure how long dogs are teenagers for but Jak was still hardly able to go in any room other than the kitchen even at seventeen months of age. It really has to be a small, small world for a naughty Collie!

Vicki had also shown me how to talk Jak through on lead distractions with the help of a pen full of duck. The first time Vicki walked Jak past the pen the ducks were in Jak reacted and immediately Vicki responded with: "Silly dog! Barking at ducks.....you don't even know what ducks are...no threat to you". The second time walking past there was no reaction: "Great work Jak nice duck walking!" Vicki rewarded Jak with her language, both body language and verbal, letting him know that she was pleased.

It sounds funny, but I could instantly see, that just by saying what you mean, Jak was able to understand what made you pleased and what didn't by the tone of voice and the body language.

I knew then I was in for some long and crazy conversations.

Lambing and Farm Life

Thinking that I would definitely need access to some sheep in the future, I booked myself on to a day long lambing course at Kate's Country School in Wales. This was a real high spot for me. Of course, Jak had to stay at home with my long beleaguered husband so that I was free and could enjoy adult company and the lovely farm. It was like a holiday for me. I did not want to come home and pick up the mantle of training Jak daily again.

Within ten minutes of arriving at the farm and getting my wellington boots and overalls on I was holding a newborn lamb that was not feeding. I was taught how to tube feed the tiny creature and watched as the lamb changed from listless and cold to warm and raring to go. Later in the day I examined a Ewe who was in labour and then delivered the lamb (normal presentation, just a big single lamb). This was such a wonderful experience.

Over the course of the day I also learned to strip colostrum from the Ewes, bottle feed and dock tails or castrate lambs as required. I got to experience learning how to move anxious Mother Ewes and their twin lambs from their bonding pens to barns some distance away. This was real fun as well as being hard work and it felt like a great achievement to see the little sheep family in their new clean environment. There were about eight of us on the course and we moved about twenty Ewes in total.

So I really loved it. It definitely made me want to move to the countryside and live like that although I knew that at this point this was really not a feasible option. I kept thinking about how Jak would be running loose around a farmyard. Would this solve his anxiety or would he spend the days barking at swinging gates and noisy animals? It was impossible to tell.

Later in the year I decided to return to Kate's Country School to spend the day getting further farming experience. With coffee and cakes to start off and then dinner and coffee at lunchtime all in the Farmhouse kitchen around a big kitchen table. I loved it so much.

If only there was a financial benefit to starting a small farm I would have been very keen to get started with some sort of farming. On this second course I was able to experience a lot of different activities, including sheep moving, feeding young calves and talking about geese, chickens and turkeys.

Back at home, I arranged with a local farmer for me to get some further experience helping him move sheep and also with his lambing. The farm was just a few hundred metres away from my home and we agreed that I would check the lambing ewes at 11pm, 2am and 5am for the weeks that they were lambing. This was a very exciting time for me.

When the night time lambing started I really enjoyed it. To be honest, even the nights that nothing happened, I really loved going out under the stars and walking through the sheep.

My life, at this time, often seemed to consist of just Jak, work and sleep so it was like a holiday to be doing something rural. I did find that three times a night is a lot of missed sleep and it was the 2am shift that seemed the most difficult to get up for. I loved the walk in the quietness of the night and I especially loved the warmth and smell of hay in the barn where the ewes were.

My skills, obviously, were minimal and I was always anxious about not seeing something important. I really did not want to be more of a nuisance than help to the farmer. I just climbed into the pens and tried to make sure no ewes were visibly about to give birth and if there were any signs of water bag or hooves protruding I phoned the farmer and he came very quickly to deal with the situation. I loved being there as the lambs were born and just marvelled at the beauty of nature.

It was a great way for me to get some lambing experience and maybe in my future there will be some farming for me. I would like to think so. Thank you Eamonn for giving me the opportunity!

Because the lambing had been so fabulous, even if I was a bit tired during the day, I decided to continue looking into sheepdog training for Jak. Maybe if he had herding to focus on and, if he could do it well, the issues we were having with other things would fade. Looking back now it seems like a very long shot but I guess I was still feeling very desperate about the Jak situation.

Distance Learning

I had spoken to my vet about having Jak neutered. The advice on ages now to be so varied. The vet said she, personally, would neuter Jak now. But, one of the benefits she listed was that Jak would stay looking like a teenager rather than growing mature physically. You may remember that I had loved the look of Jak's Sire. So I decided to try to put neutering off until Jak was older unless I really needed to have it done to see if it helped to calm him.

I then emailed a different sheepdog trainer and asked about a two hour assessment to see if Jak and I could train together this year before he was 12 months old. In the event this assessment session did not work out but the trainer directed me to another sheepdog trainer further north who took dogs in for an assessment over the course of a fortnights residential stay for the dog.

I thought that this may be a great way to have Jak assessed as I was still either out at work or in the kitchen with him constantly and having no dog free breaks at all. I often felt physically and emotionally drained and the break for me would be great too.

At this point in time Jak seemed to have suddenly become a little bit more mature and was possibly beginning to listen more. He was still completely wild but it seemed like there may be just the beginnings of some improvement!

I was still really keen for Jak to go and test his Sheepdog ability. I can remember wondering if Mizzle was keen to herd sheep when she was at this age so obviously it must be something that I felt I needed to know. I was not too concerned about the outcome. It would be cheaper and easier if Jak was not interested in working with sheep or did not have the required skills.

If he did have a great herding gene and became trained to work with sheep, then possibly there would be an opportunity to work with him in Eamonn's sheep fields.

This would provide exercise a couple of days a week as well as give me the chance to check on the sheep. I knew it would be seasonal. There was no way that I would take Jak into a field with pregnant ewes in!

I knew that I would miss Jak if he went away as it seemed like we were just starting a more relaxed relationship at this point. Equally, though, I was desperately in need of a break from the intense and emotional daily hard work of constantly looking after and training Jak. So Jak was duly booked in to be assessed by the Sheepdog trainer up north starting on Easter Sunday.

I was very sad to see Jak go, but I looked forward to the break and I knew that Jak would have time to try out with the sheep in a controlled environment. At this point I was not sure which would suit me better. If I were to find out that Jak was an expert, and so needed access to sheep to train with, there could be financial commitments for me to make. Training was not cheap. Perhaps it would be better if Jak was not interested in herding sheep.

In that case I would be able to look at other activities to share with him. I already knew that although Jak could jump great heights and loved jumping he would never cope with the excitement or the presence of the other dogs at agility training or competitions.

Although I did have to find some money to pay for Jak to try out for the two weeks, I was happy that this gave Jak the chance to fulfil any inherited talent he may have had. Even if Jak were talented and needed to stay for the full eight weeks he would still only be ten months old when he came home.

Whilst Jak was away, I discovered that now I really, really missed him. I could not remember what I used to do with all the free time I must have had before Jak came into my life. Despite all his naughtiness I realised that I felt much more connected to life when Jak was around.

As it turned out at the end of the fortnight the sheepdog trainer got back to me to say that Jak just did not have the concentration to herd sheep although he was a lovely dog.

Apparently Jak had been very distracted in the trial training sessions with the sheep and he had not listened to the trainer nor had he made any progress over the days he was there. I made the plan to come and bring Jak home.

On the day I collected him the trainer spent almost an hour giving me some more advice and some training with the lead to help me control Jak better. She explained that Jak had really not engaged with her in training sessions and shown little interest in working with the sheep. Part of me was sad for Jak but I understood exactly what the trainer was saying.

This trainer also recommended that I should keep Jak's world small until he started listening to me and doing what I asked him to do. She recommended keeping Jak restricted or on the lead and constantly asking him to sit or lie down when walking so that he always had something to be responding to.

She felt that Jak was a real 'Jack the Lad' and actually I could not agree more. So I resolved, yet again, to be much tougher with Jak. The idea behind him being more restrained was about Jak working out for himself who was in charge and how his behaviour had to be.

I had learned from many books that repeated behaviour gets ingrained and by me continuing to allow Jak to misbehave on walks this behaviour was being reinforced as his default outdoor conduct. Perhaps a complete break from that repeatedly negative routine by keeping Jak's world really small again would help everything. I really hoped so. Life was still truly hard.

Life was also emotionally difficult keeping Jak more contained and obedient. I felt sorry for him and I missed our hugs and cuddles together. But I did know that somehow Jak's behaviour had to improve.

I really did not want Jak to end up being a big, totally out of control, monster and so far this was the only way our pathway seemed to be leading.

Home Struggles

By May, I was feeling beaten again, sad and hopeless. Jak was much calmer, but only because he was in his new larger pen I had built. Anytime Jak was out in the garden he was on the lead and behaving. He was not happy although there were definitely starting to be some positive results.

Within just a couple of weeks Jak had learned to lie at my feet on the lead for over ten minutes. This was unprecedented behaviour, but somehow the sparkle had gone out of Jak's eyes and I was not happy either. Life was calmer and, of course I could leave the kitchen as Jak was now contained. It did feel like I was not interacting with Jak though, and as soon as I took him out on a walk his anxiety was back immediately.

When I tried relaxing the being contained in his pen, or the being on the lead obeying every command Jak took advantage straight away. He had been so good at laying down at my feet several times a day that one day I let him sit in front of me and stroked his head and spoke to him. The rest of that day Jak refused to sit or lie down when told.

It really did seem to be all or nothing. Either me being totally strict all day, every day or Jak doing whatever he felt like. There seemed to be no leeway in this at all. So I was sad that I wasn't getting to spend as much time with Jak as I had in the past. I could see that the trainer's method was working and that I would have to stay strict. I did feel guilty though. I did not know anyone else who treated their dog this way.

Every time I relaxed the regime in any way Jak took advantage. He quickly learned that tipping over his water bowl got some attention but other than that he did slowly start being more responsive.

Outside in the garden on the lead Jak had started to try and do as he was told. The fact that he was starting to listen and he was trying to do what I asked was a new concept. I could see him really trying to keep calm when he was asked to lie down.

Sometimes Jak was particularly good in that he had been able to lie down for about ten minutes with me whilst in the garden. Even when he had seen other family members walking through the conservatory and coming towards us, he had wriggled but still managed to keep calm for another couple of minutes.

Towards the end of May, when Jak was nine months old, I could see some more improvement. I was able to sit out on the garden bench in the sunshine whilst Jak lay nicely on his lead. The length of time was getting ever longer and Jak started to be able to control himself when there were small distractions like a bumble bee buzzing past or when a pigeon flew over.

Was this the start of a more controlled user friendly Jak? I certainly hoped so. It was a lovely few moments and so nice to see Jak behaving like the dog I had wanted to take camping and hiking with me. And I noticed that Jak really had grown into a beautiful looking dog.

There were lots of emotional ups and downs during this time with Jak. The strict regime was certainly working, but it was so slow! My logical thoughts said that Jak would only really be able to go back out into the world after his hormones were settled and he had been neutered but that was even now some months away.

I was still stalling the neutering as I was anxious about the vet stating that dogs stop developing emotionally as well as physically when they are neutered so therefore they may be more immature if they have not finished maturing before they have the operation.

This was a cause for concern for me as I knew that Jak needed some maturity to deal with his 'Jak the Lad' issues. I purposely did not want to have him neutered until he was at least one year old. That was August, a full four months away.

At this time I was finding many countryside walks in our area and learning my way around footpaths through country parks on my own without Jak. As we tend to move around the country quite a lot for our ministry we are always living in new places. This means that I have to make time to seek out the best dog walking opportunities each time after we have moved.

Walking without Jak felt wrong. This was what I had planned for us to do together. By June I had discovered miles of woodland and lake paths I could access from my house, not even needing the car to get there. But jak was not able to come with me.

If only I could help Jak to get over his walking issues this exercise would be great for him. I felt very despondent that I had found all these great woods and paths just on my doorstep whilst Jack was still in restricted rehab!

From a small puppy, barking had always been an issue with Jak. It was all attention seeking or an early attempt at communicating with us. But it was loud and sometimes very persistent.

Some mornings, Jak was barking when we left the kitchen, but when we left the house, he stopped the barking immediately when he heard the front door slam. Obviously he had decided that everyone had left. I was so cross with this behavior. It seemed a clear sign of attention seeking. But I was at a loss as to how to stop it.

Some weeks later I started taking Jak down to work with me on Saturdays when no one else was there. It meant that I had access to a big enclosed area. I was able to try to do some obedience training in the big hall. I had done this before for a few weeks some time ago and we had both enjoyed it. This was the first time he was free in such a large space for a long time.

Jak was superb. He did all his Lie Downs and Stays for a long time. And all without treats too. Then I made him lie down and watch while I put out four rows of small plastic chairs for him to jump over and we did a bit of agility. I just gave him fuss as a reward, no treats.

We both really loved the time spent doing this and I was on a high. It was great to spend some fun time working with Jak. But when we got back home Jak became really noisy and tried to escape from his pen all day long. I certainly didn't feel like I could do this every week if Jak was going to be so disturbed and naughty afterwards.

Within the next seventy two hours Jak had managed to get out of his pen four times. Twice when either we forgot to bolt the door properly or he managed to unbolt it and twice Jak actually broke through the wood of the door.

In Jak's defence, at the time he physically broke through the door, we were hosing the lawn which had always been a source of great excitement for him. Jak loved to leap up and try to catch the water. A fun and very wet, game.

Jak was not unwilling to go back in his pen when we caught him after his escapes. In fact, Jak was never bothered about going in his crate or the pen. This was such a good thing. I would have hated to have to force him somewhere he did not want to go.

I did think that fluctuating hormones affected us both. Jak was still unable to control himself when his tail was waving high above him, curled over his back and when he had that glint in his eye. In fact, Jak was always much calmer when he just looked like nice puppy Jak instead of a wild eyed and hairy werewolf!!

At this point in time I was really at a mental and physical low. I could not get Jak the exercise his growing body needed each day and I had no realistic long term exercise plans for the future. All the things that Jak would excel at physically involved other dogs and people and it was beginning to be more and more obvious that he just could not handle this at all. I did not know which way to turn.

Whilst Jak had been away I had read a book that described how a Collie learnt the names to over one thousand toys! This seemed like a possibility for another new game to play. Perhaps it would keep Jak's brain busy. So I went toy shopping.

I bought a whole stack of new toys for Jak and put them together in a box writing their names on them with a marker pen. I hoped that fetching toys by name might be another 'job' that I could get Jak to do.

I tried repeatedly playing this game with Jak each morning. I just used a small selection of the toys so that Jak could learn the names. But I felt that, although Jak did know the name for the toy I was asking him to fetch, and he did know which toy I wanted he was choosing to bring a different one. Making up his own game to his rules yet again.

Sometimes Jak even ran directly to the toy I had asked for and touched it with his nose but then he gave me a really cheeky look before picking up a different toy and running away. It was clear that bringing named toys was not high on Jak's agenda of daytime activities.

I was still struggling the the ongoing fact that whenever Jak was out of his crate, he needed me to be present in the kitchen. Not because he was destructive like so many other difficult dogs are, but because he continually barked and threw himself against the windows and the doors incessantly.

If Jak was not barking he might be trying to dig out imagined shadows in the tiled floor. Or pestering Jessie even if she was in her safety pen. In fact, unless I was constantly training Jak to do tricks or obedience training with treats I could not distract him from doing these things.

Katy still felt that the lack of exercise was the main reason for my problems. She thought that if I could get to have Jak running free for a couple of hours a day he would settle down at home. The logic was sound. Every dog book, particularly collie books agreed. But I was not sure. The more I took Jak outside of the house the more unsettled he seemed to be at home. And perhaps unsettled was the wrong word, the more distressed he became maybe, or wound up? Whatever it was I was not having much luck in tracking it down.

Excitability had always been one of Jak's big problems. It built up, one excitement after another, with no calming down in between.

I could remember that even on his first walks when he would see a person, then a dog, then a bird and then fetching his toy and then a treat… it all built up until he was uncontrollable and snapping and biting my clothes. Not even really thinking clearly in the moment. What on earth would the future hold?

Mizzle and Tulla

In March Katy had told me that Mizzle had been mated with a lovely Border Collie. So the family were hoping for puppies. We both researched all these things and had long chats about how many puppies it could be. Personally, I was thinking that by the time a large clutch of puppies was nearly ready to go to their new home Katy's house might be as chaotic as mine was with Jak. A thought that made me smile.

By early April Mizzle was looking fatter and acting very lethargic. The usual scan was booked with the vet for mid-April and we all waited patiently for news. There was really bad news at the scan. Apparently dogs can absorb their puppies sometimes in pregnancy and it looked exactly as if this had happened with Mizzle. This was a most upsetting event.

All of the family were devastated and so upset for Mizzle that she had become pregnant and now nothing was going to happen.All the puppy plans were halted and the family tried to get back to life as usual. There would only really be one more chance for Mizzle to have a first litter because of her age.

Everyone was sad about events and there were still issues to be resolved. Mizzle had a further appointment at the vets to check if everything was returning to normal. I received a sudden telephone call after the vet appointment. The vet had performed another scan and found that Mizzle was still carrying one puppy! This news was obviously joyful.

But Katy told me that having one puppy was bad for dogs, especially first time bitches. I did a bit of research and discovered that one puppy tends to grow very large and the bitch often cannot give birth to the puppy naturally.

This proved to be the case with Mizzle and a caesarean section was scheduled. Emotions were running high. No one had planned for Mizzle to have such a large operation. And what about the health of the puppy?

Again, it was a waiting game. The Caesarean was scheduled for 10th May, a Friday. Soon after midday I got the news. It was a large girl. Both the Mother and the puppy were doing well. Phew. All sorted we thought somewhat prematurely!

The next day Katy was back in touch. Mizzle had declined to take up her Motherly role. It appeared that she did not recognise the puppy as hers at all. This can be a common reaction in bitches who do not give birth naturally. It was worrying though.

Although the puppy was large by new born measurements she was actually still really tiny and human care was no substitute for a canine Mother's touch. After a few hours it appeared that Katy and the family were getting the hang of it all. The puppy had a cloth to cuddle under and when she cried Mizzle was brought in to (reluctantly) feed the baby.

Then after the puppy had fed enough the human carer had to wipe the puppy's bottom with a wet cloth to simulate the bitch licking the puppy to stimulate eliminating waste products. Obviously this process had to continue night and day until the puppy was weaned. It was a very tiring job and emotionally stressful too. The responsibility of keeping a tiny puppy alive and well seemed huge.

Looking after Mizzle was a worrying business too. Obviously she still had to recuperate from the operation and she seemed very distressed when the puppy cried. Was this because she didn't understand? Was it jealousy? Would the two dogs ever get along with a rocky start like this?

At first Mizzle seemed so anxious when the puppy cried, but quite soon she did start to take an interest in the wet cloth bottom wiping. Within a week she was trying to help - and also beginning to show nesting behaviour.

I found it quite sad that the caesarean operation had stopped the normal whelping hormones but it was really good news that Mizzle was catching up with things now. Although we all worried about the situation, Mizzle came through as the star she always has been.

Within a short space of time Mizzle was being a real Mum, feeding, washing and listening out for the tiny pup who was growing rapidly. This was really turning out to be a lovely story after all the ups and downs.

The puppy was given the name of Tulla. Very quickly Tulla started to put on weight and turned from a fat sausage shape into a plump puppy. Sometimes when she rolled over onto her back she struggled to get up because of the big tummy she was getting.

It seemed no time at all until Tulla was the length of a ruler and starting to look more like a little dog than a large sausage. Tulla's markings were very similar to Mizzle's and as the family got to handle her more the question came up 'what now'? If there had been a litter of six puppies they would have all been found new homes, but this puppy was special.

It soon became clear that Tulla was going to stay. After all the emotions and worries and the nights spent staying up to feed her everyone felt so bonded with her. No other home would do.

I wondered if Tulla would turn out to be hard work like Jak but even though she did try to escape from her pen and crate sometimes she was always more placid than Jak - and already listening, learning and trying to please Katy at an early age.

I did like hearing from Katy that Tulla disrupted their organised home now and then. From time to time there were reports of Tulla driving Mizzle mad and Mizzle needing to shelter in her crate for a break. There were also occasional issues of the dogs scrapping and snapping at each other but as Tulla grew these diminished naturally.

Katy reported on all her long walks with the two dogs as soon as Tulla was old enough to do the big field walking. By the end of July, Tulla's training was still going well. Of course, training started for Tulla as soon as she was aware of her surroundings and Mizzle, of course, portrayed, how a well behaved dog lived life!

As Tulla grew, the time was coming for Jak and Tulla to meet. I had a lot of reservations.

I felt that Katy would want to protect Tulla from Jak's overzealous, boisterous playing! But in the end, when the dogs did meet, Jak played very excitedly with Tulla all day and late into the evening without seeming able to stop. And they both seemed to thoroughly enjoy the time spent together. It also gave Mizzle a break from a rowdy and enthusiastic Tulla.

This time spent together did show that Tulla and Jak were both very energetic dogs. Mizzle seemed pleased to be able to rest on the sofa.

We managed several visits after this first stay and of course with Jak being neutered in mid-September there would be no risk of surprise naughty part Welsh puppies appearing on the scene!

Further Training

After many distressing emails to Katy about Jak during the beginning of 2019, Katy offered to put me in touch with Gilliana, a trainer near to Katy's home that Katy and Mizzle had met previously. Jak and I were due to visit Katy's and so the appointment was arranged and Jak had a new trainer to meet.

Gilliana was lovely and Jak was obviously quite in awe of her presence straight away, being very obedient. But when we walked just a little way up the road Jak kicked off big time, at a car, then a dog walker and then at a person walking. I could see that Gilliana was horrified at Jak's terrible out of control behaviour.

We returned to Katy's garden and the training began. Gilliana took the lead and trained Jak to lie down nicely on a dog bed raised on metal legs. Jak managed it very well. He certainly knew what he was supposed to be doing.

It was only when I took the lead that Jak started misbehaving, jumping straight off when I walked away and even snapping at the lead or my hands when I took him back. It was clear to everyone there that my relationship with Jak was not what it should be.

Gilliana gave me as much advice as she was able to in our limited time, she showed me how to loop Jak's lead in a figure of eight over his nose to have a bit more control over him and she promised to keep in touch online so that I could ask for specific advice as I needed it. I was truly grateful for all her help.

As Jak was growing bigger the disruption to every part of life at home was also getting bigger. In the weeks following this lesson some things did improve with Jak. If I put the lead over his nose as well as round his neck whilst at home he did settle down somewhat and was able to lie down even in the lounge for a short time.

Any respite from Jak's continual bombardment and barking was really welcome. But when I tried to take Jak outdoors with the lead looped over his nose, he jumped in the air and did huge somersaults high in the air until the lead dislodged and he could wriggle free. The acrobatics were certainly very impressive but safety close to the road was an issue. Therefore the looped lead never became an option for outside walking.

I bought a dog bed with legs similar to the one that Gilliana had used and Jak knew straight away what I wanted him to do. But unless I stood immediately in front of the bed he constantly disobeyed me and made it hard work for me to get him back in place. If I took a step away he chewed either the lead or the bed and in just a couple of days there was no bed left. Just a metal frame. This happened with two similar beds over the next three months.

Gilliana kept her word and whenever I contacted her when I was despairing, she gave me great advice. After much effort on my part I seemed able to keep the kitchen a more peaceful place. But training wise or on walks I was absolutely no further forward.

Jak was still doing really well at obedience and agility in the large enclosed Hall that I had access to. We both enjoyed the sessions but Jak was always hyper excited after we had spent time training there. I was never sure wether this was excitement or anxiety from being outside the safety of home.

Jak was good at all types of 'tricks' and 'tasks' if there were food rewards at the end of them. I could put Jak in a Down at one end of the Hall and walk a complete circuit or even go out of the door and come back whilst he lay patiently waiting not moving at all and looking so beautiful, the faithful dog I always wanted. Again, his Sit and Recall were both perfect.

The tricks Jak knew at this stage were also awesome. Jak would do a figure of eight around my legs with great excitement and as I have only been blessed with short legs and Jak was getting tall it looked so funny. One of my favourite things.

Jak could pick up lots of rubber chickens one by one and put them in a basket to the command 'Chicken in the Basket'. He was also able to put all of his toys into their storage box to the command of 'Jak - In the Box'. I really could not understand why he was so attentive and obedient at these tasks and yet still so totally unruly out on walks.

Katy wrote to me in response to an email about this question. She felt that it was really good for Jak to have things to think about and to work on. Katy was, even now, under the impression that if I persevered and got Jak as much exercise as possible that he would eventually work it out and start enjoying walks. I could not agree. I saw no hope of this happening despite the fact that I was managing to walk him every day. Not all walks had an aggressive episode in them. But most did.

Nearly all the advice I read in books or saw online confirmed that naughty dogs needed more exercise. But it just did not seem that more excursions outdoors were helpful. The more walks I took Jak on the higher his anxiety and stress levels seemed to be and the worse his behaviour was at home.

At nearly a year old we still never ever saw Jak lie down and sleep unless he was in his crate. He was still constantly jumping up everyone and onto everything and barking nearly all the time. When our older dog, Jessie, was out of her 'protective custody' pen Jak pestered her mercilessly until she turned and started to fight with him.

I was so tired. I could see no end to this day to day battle with Jak and I wondered how it would all end. I felt sure that eventually it would end in someone being seriously bitten by Jak and him having to be put to sleep. The thought kept me awake at night...but I still could not see any solution.

Day by day I was reading any books that had ideas, training or tricks in and tried everything new I read. I also looked online and read copious amounts of dog owners and trainers tips on Facebook.

I felt beaten, but I was not willing to give in. I was so sure that under it all Jak was a good dog and that it was me who was unable to find the way to lead him into decent behaviour.

I often just sat in Jak's pen with him crying into his long fur praying that I would find a way to make this all work without breaking Jak's spirit.

Anxiety

Meanwhile, my health was suffering. I was at that awkward stage of life where a woman's body doesn't know what is going on and emotions and hormones are fluctuating wildly. Added to that was the stress of working through the fact that Jak did not want to leave the house. Getting Jak had been my 'get out in the fresh air more often' plan, and so I was struggling mentally.

I had to find other ways to get outdoors and to do things that gave me my confidence back. I took a day to go out test riding a couple of cheap motorbikes. Riding an unknown bike in an unknown area reminded me what an accomplished motorbike rider I had become over the years. I loved it.

I wondered vaguely if Jak would ever be up for a sidecar on my motorbike. But I knew straight away that he would hate the sight of strange people near him and unknown dogs. No, it was clear that motor biking would have to happen on my own. This made me so sad. Another hobby, like the hiking, and the camping that I could not share with Jak.

Looking back from a point where Jak is now over eighteen months old and much more mature I believe that a lot of the early problems were completely linked to communication. Somehow, perhaps through the issue and problem of walking outdoors, we had missed an opportunity to learn what each other wanted.

Certainly today, Jak tells me far more about what he wants to do and what he will only do very unwillingly, and so we seem to understand each other better.

The fact that in these difficult 'teenage months' for Jak we were both battling with anxiety, I believe, made both of us worse.

For example, when I walked Jak he was nervous of noises, loud trucks, people shouting, doors slamming and dogs barking. Because I quickly learned that Jak always reacted in these situations I also became anxious when I heard those dogs, people and traffic knowing that Jak was tensing up.

This obviously, was really counter-productive. The more anxious I was the more anxious Jak became and the more likely he was to react if anyone came near us. The longer these issues continued the more inventive I had to become.

Once I had realised that I was getting anxious out walking when I heard a dog barking in the distance or people shouting, I quickly discovered that by playing Dolly Parton tracks through my headphones loudly I was unable to hear the noises around us.

This meant that I could just keep on striding out confidently encouraging Jak to do the same. Thank you Dolly for all the positive songs that helped me to climb out of my anxiety!

At this time I was really hoping that Jak would start applying the more calm behaviour I was seeing at home to reactions to dogs when we were out. But, it seemed that the moment we left the 'safety' of home Jak was fearful and looking for dogs constantly even far off in the distance.

Jak did not even look like the same dog once we left the house with his whole body posture changing. Being outdoors was obviously a very severe issue for him. Then suddenly a new symptom of Jak's anxiety started.

Shadow chasing became another problem to deal with. One day after Jak had a gallop around at the hall, like a switch going on, Jak became obsessed with shadow chasing. When I researched this issue I discovered that it was a stressed Collie symptom. I couldn't believe it. If this had come on slowly, perhaps we could have dealt with it. On the Saturday Jak did not seem interested in shadows but from early on the Sunday morning he couldn't stop finding them and was working himself up into a real frenzy over them.

I blamed myself a lot for the shadow chasing. Jak was not being exercised enough, he was not being mentally challenged enough and so on. Thankfully, I had seen some normal, crazy Jak type behaviour at times, so I knew that the old Jak was still in there.

Part of me also did suspect that this was all an exceptionally clever type of attention seeking behaviour as Jak only chased shadows at first when we were there...but he did seem very obsessed. Within just a few days this habit had intensified. Nothing was distracting Jak from his shadow chasing.

If left alone Jak would just chase shadows, whether real, visible ones or unseen, imagined ones until he was exhausted. He would yip and squeal loudly with excitement the whole time. Even scratching and digging at the floor tiles or the wall plaster trying to dig out things he was chasing.

After a few day I had to bring his old crate out for him to sleep in at night. It felt like such a big backwards step. Since coming back from the residential sheepdog training Jak had just slept in a bigger pen built in under the stairs.

However, with Jak safely in the crate overnight and the crate covered with a blanket, there were no shadows to chase and Jak started sleeping again so that he was no longer tired and stressed first thing in the morning, worn out with chasing and digging all night.

I managed to have a good night's sleep too. I was also very relieved to read in a book that all Collies can start rounding up shadows when they discover the game. So possibly I had not made this happen by not solving the exercise issue. Although, obviously, boredom can play a big part.

Jak still chases shadows now, although he has learned to do it more quietly. And he can be distracted from it.

Jak loves sunny days and knows exactly where to look for that beam of sunlight falling on the floor or the reflected gleam on the patio as the french doors are opened. Once the sun shining in the window was reflecting off the engraved name tag on his collar and Jak played with that for ages. Only food time distracted him from this.

I still keep watching Jak and trying to see if he is happy and playful or anxiously chasing off threats. Jak is definitely more calm on an overcast day. Walking in the garden in the dark of winter has also proved to be challenging.

We had an automatic light that came on when the dogs went out into the garden. It lit up the path and the lawn. But Jak started to see this as a shadow provider. He could not focus on doing his 'business' he just ran around excitedly yipping and chasing. We tried turning the light off and using a torch but this was even worse. Jak could not walk straight for bouncing and chasing the moving circle of light.

This was bad news for walks too because I had always thought that if things got bad enough I would walk Jak at three or four in the morning. But now I knew that this would not be possible in the dark because of the shadow chasing.

So, regarding the shadow chasing, Jak was obsessed in the summer because of the rays of sunshine. And he was obsessed in the winter because of the dark, finding chinks of light under doors and between curtains. Like other Jak issues, there seemed to be no solution for this.

Hannah from Canissimo

I was still very upset and stressed and desperate to do something to make Jak's life, and the lives of my family happier. Jak had produced so many difficult issues which had to be dealt with or lived with and so few of these issues had been resolved over the months.

Home was still a really stressful place to be because of Jak's behaviour. No one else from the family wanted to spend any time in the kitchen with Jak and I, and to be honest, being in the kitchen with Jak was often unrewarding and tiring for me too.

Happily Gilliana, the trainer from Warwickshire, messaged me late one Saturday night saying that she had found the details of a trainer local to me who may be able to help with Jak. And so, yet another trainer was booked in and I found yet another sum of money to spend on Jak. I honestly believed that I could have bought a 'Crufts Best in Show Champion' dog for all the money I had now spent on Jak and still my problems were nowhere near being solved!

Friday came around, the day of the first new training session. I met with Hannah, the new trainer. I had taken a leap of faith and paid for a course of five sessions with Hannah and I was relieved to have something to hope for!

I had been keeping Jak with the door of his crate open all the time I was in the kitchen and I had done lots of daily training. Frisbee throwing and anything I could think of to distract him, but Jak still preferred to be in his pen chasing shadows or loose in the kitchen chasing shadows. Jak was also still objecting to having any sort of lead on and becoming noisy and vicious looking as soon as we left the house for whichever type of daily walk.

I was also completely stressed with the whole situation. If only I had been able to get the walking issues resolved before this point. There were so many long walks I could have taken Jak on where he could have run off the lead for long stretches too. But even just getting to the walking places without Jak going completely berserk was impossible. Controlling Jak on the lead when he had an outburst was also impossible. He was now so tall and strong. It was impossible for me to physically keep control of him.

I was feeling very embarrassed about the state Jak was in and my inability to cope. The new training sessions with Hannah started in June. Jak was ten months old. Hannah was superb. She managed to appear as if Jak's issues were a normal thing and that there would be a solution of some kind if we persevered.

In the very first training session, Hannah suggested that we took Jak out for a walk using two aids to help change his behaviour. Firstly, a rucksack that Jak wore with a small bottle of water in each side and secondly using a prong collar.

Prong collars are much vilified online and later that evening when I researched these I found that nearly everybody advised against them. When I first saw the collar I panicked myself. It looked terrible. But, by this stage of the game, I had to try anything that might work because re-homing Jak just was not a reasonable prospect with his behaviour issues and his ready nipping, growling and aggressive behaviour. I had to find a way to cope or the outlook for Jak was very poor.

This very first training session with Hannah was a game changer. It was also the start of a whole new era with Jak. A much more positive time. Jak responded to Hannah's self-confident training really well and even on that first day Jak was able to walk with us both around the neighbourhood and, although he looked worried, Jak walked without reacting to people we passed and dogs at a distance.

This was really ground breaking. And a great starting point for our five sessions working together. I continued walking Jak with the prong collar and rucksack at least once every day until our second session. This time, Hannah brought her dog with her and we did some work together getting Jak to walk past Hannah and her dog. Jak was nervous, but he did manage to walk properly.

I then had some weeks to practice what we had learned. I continued taking Jak out once or twice a day on the lead using the prong collar and the rucksack. We had some good days and some bad days.

One evening, as we rounded a blind corner not far from our house, Jak and I bumped straight into a lady walking a really huge silver and white Husky. Jak kicked off immediately. Jumping up on his back legs growling, snapping and snarling and the Husky responded by lunging back at us. Thankfully, the road next to us was clear of traffic, and I was able to manhandle Jak across the road. I was shaking and very upset.

Even with the added control of the prong collar and the distraction of the rucksack I would not be able to keep Jak under control. Again, I felt that this would eventually end in Jak being out of control and result in him being put down.

I still did not understand why Jak attacked other dogs. When Jak had been introduced to other dogs in safe environments he had got on with all the dogs he met with the exception of Jessie who had instigated fighting every time they met. The Jak I knew at home was a fun loving cute dog even though he was so unruly and naughty.

A few days later there was some good news concerning the big Husky. On seeing him being walked several days later the owner encouraged me to put Jak into a Sit and she got the Husky to sit and we chatted about reactive dogs and how to deal with them. We also discussed the intolerance of other dog walkers who shouted at us and increased the tension of the situation.

It was good to hear that this dog owner had experienced some of what I was under pressure with.

I was really grateful to this lady. Her patience showed me over the many days that we met that Jak could sit and calm down and not be reactive when he recognised a dog on walks.

Different Experiences

In one of the training sessions with Hannah, we walked through a busy town centre. Jak walked perfectly, although he did seem to be surprised at the amount of people and the unusual noises and sights there. Jak did not react at all until we were back in the car park and a small Terrier dog came close to him. Jak leapt up angrily barking and actually bit my hand redirecting his angry reaction onto me.

Another day Jak and I joined a pack walk with Hannah and a good number of dogs. Jak was able to do this walk behaving quite well but his body language showed how uncomfortable he was with the situation. I noted that if dogs who were approaching us walked nicely, and were well controlled, he could walk by. But if the dog approaching was anxious or pulling on the lead Jak always lunged out noisily.

On our walks from home I started encouraging Jak to scent mark to order, hoping that he would enjoy marking things and so start to enjoy his walks. I walked Jak down to 'popular lamp posts' and then up to the road sign at the top of our road. Once there I encouraged him to sniff as sniffing is supposed to be calming as well as tiring.

I was also thinking that if Jak really liked sniffing and marking some territory he may start to look forward to his walks and be less nervous. The day we got to the road sign on the corner of our road and the main road I celebrated when Jak was able to give the road sign a big doggy signature whilst keeping his tail low and calm.

I was so excited and we may have both done a little celebratory dance together before coming home that day. It did occur to me that encouraging this behaviour may cause Jak to become obsessed with scent marking which, of course, it did.

This bad habit came to a climax when my husband proudly showed me the big flat pack bookcase he had just spent a long time building and Jak took one sniff and 'christened' it thoroughly with his scent.

Thankfully scent marking issues in the home stopped a few weeks after Jak was neutered. At this time something else happened. After the neutering operation Jak took well to the Vet collar, but he did not fit in his crate with the collar on. Jak still needed to be in the crate at night as he could not shut off and sleep at all otherwise. So I purchased a vet medical vest for him that covered everything needed so that Jak could not actively get to his stitches.

Something strange happened. At bedtime, when I took off the huge lampshade collar and put on his 'pyjamas', Jak snuggled into me. Every evening, for the duration of his convalescence from the operation, after I put his pyjamas on, we cuddled together by his crate and I talked to him about the dog I hoped he would become.

This period lasted about a fortnight and then Jak was able to be walked and no longer needed the pyjamas (although I may have continued putting them on him for a few more weeks just because I liked the cuddle moments).

Because Jak liked wearing the medical vest as pyjamas I wondered if a Thunder Vest would help him while out walking. I did try this for a while, but it really had no effect on Jak's temperament and he tried to bite at the vest so I abandoned that glimmer of hope quite quickly. I had noted in an email to Katy that: 'Jak is doing well. It will be good when the Vet collar comes off but really he has not bothered about it much nor the vest. And he is being lovely and well behaved. Of course not going on long exciting walks helps his temperament as it always has.'

This was a key point and I had repeatedly missed it. Jak was lovely and cuddly and calmer at the times when I was not taking him out for a big walk each day.

After Jak's recovery from the operation I decided to change my walking pattern and to try taking him out with Jessie as their relationship had mellowed. I thought that if I took them out together each day I could just take Jak out for a long woodland walk twice a week or so and his behaviour might stay calmer.

I noted that this was about plan number 156 but I did feel that perhaps we were getting somewhere. Jak was such a lovely dog both in looks and temperament at home. If only I could cure these outside problems!

Over the next couple of months I did have some success in walking Jak around a quiet industrial estate, but although I enjoyed the walks Jak really did not seem to be able to enjoy them. He still ran and hid away when he saw his lead in my hand.

Eventually I found a walk from home where Jak had to walk down a road and then a lane to fields and woods. After a few trips to this, more secluded place, I started letting Jak off the lead again and practicing his recall as well as enjoying watching him run free. After doing this walk many, many times I noted that although Jak loved the fields and the woods, he still hated walking the distance from the house and was very anxious if we heard any other dogs even a long way off in the distance.

Indoor Training

The last session of the five that I had previously booked with Hannah was held at our house looking at Jak's indoor behaviour. This session was held in January 2020. It was almost five months since Jak had been neutered, but he had still not calmed down to any great extent at home at all. Anytime that he was out of his crate he barked, he still leapt on surfaces and was generally a hooligan.

We had, even now, not seen Jak lie down and sleep or even relax since he had been a tiny puppy unless he was in his pen or crate. Home had been chaos forever and Jak showed no signs of changing his behaviour in the house at all.

We could not identify whether this bad behaviour stemmed from anxiety or whether Jak really just was some sort of crazy dog. Jak slept quietly every night only barking if he heard the cat flap clicking. But all day and every evening until bedtime Jak was busy.

If I was not keeping him occupied with training and treats, Jak was pestering Jessie through the door of her pen or chasing shadows. If Jak caught sight of a person, outdoors in the next garden or through a window, he erupted into a loud and uncontrollable manic barking and jumping session. Jak was always quick enough to get away from any hands put out to catch his collar and rein him in.

This was frustrating for me and became an amusing game for Jak. I was still needing to keep him on a long lead tied to me a lot of the time I was in the house. It was not good for either of us.

Hannah and I discussed trying an e-collar. I took plenty of time to do a lot of research and discovered that these collars were going to be banned at some point in the United Kingdom. The bill had been passed in parliament to ban them but a date had not yet been set.

This made me nervous as well as reading all the negative press about this type of training aid. Hannah showed me that the collar was able to just vibrate. An electric current did not have to be used.

I tried the collar in my hand and felt just a very weak buzz, a mild vibrating action nothing more. I could not see that this would help anything but I was willing to try it out and see what happened. The result from this one product was like a miracle taking place. Jak responded immediately to the brief buzz of the collar.

Within a week Jak's behaviour at home had changed. He seemed to suddenly understand that we did not want lunging at the table or the door and that chasing the cat was unacceptable behaviour. Wild barking for long stretches of time was stopped quickly.

Before the end of January a milestone was reached. Jak spent an entire day out of his crate and not on the lead whilst in the house. I could hardly believe it. Jak did not wear the collar all day, just for a while each day when his behaviour was at its worst.

What I believe the collar did, that we had previously not been able to achieve, was communicate with Jak. The correction from a distance was able to show him clearly what behaviour was acceptable and what behaviour was not.

Jak was happy and relaxed in between the use of the collar, in fact, when I had to buzz the collar Jak looked round more as if it were an annoyance to him rather than a punishment. I believe that this proved that a big part of my problem with Jak had always been communication.

I remembered that I had read a book that suggested that some dogs respond much better to body language than words and I started being purposeful in my daily communication with Jak.

Within a few weeks of using the e collar just to buzz Jak when he misbehaved badly a lot of things changed. Jak could sprawl out in the conservatory in the sunshine and sleep. Jak was able to curl up in his bed in the kitchen and relax.

Jak did become collar sensitive for a time, behaving well when he was wearing it but still 'trying it on' when he was not wearing the collar, but over the weeks his good behaviour became more usual than his naughty behaviour.

As Jak got older, now we could communicate better, his bad conduct in the kitchen improved. At one time we could never leave any food on the worktops or on the dining table. Now Jak was able to ignore human food distractions.

This meant that Jak could be running loose whilst we were sitting at the table eating. Granted, we often got an over energetically thrown tennis ball arriving on the table or a chewed soft toy, but Jak no longer jumped up at us or tried to get our food.

The only exception to this better behaviour was on windy days. Like a young child, Jak was over happy and over energetic on windy days. His wide-open eager eyes darted around wildly and his full plumed tail waved high over his back. His body language showed immediately that he was uncontrollable. Perhaps this issue will fade with age. We seem to get a lot of windy days and they all seem very tiring for me.

I do especially want to thank all the trainers that helped me with Jak. It was a long and difficult journey to where we are now, and on the way there were so few successes at the time.

But looking back, each step helped me to see new things and to learn more about Jak whose personality was so complex. Some of the trainers who helped me are listed in the appendix to this book and I would personally recommend them to you if you are needing help and guidance with your dog.

Email

Hi Katy

I thought it was high time that I wrote to say THANK YOU for encouraging me to get Crazy Jak. As you know it has been a tremendously difficult journey over the last 15 months but because of Jak's needs I have had to get to find myself and to start believing in myself again. Probably something that I have not done since 2012 and maybe earlier!

This week we have just walked in the woods near home, our favourite spot. Today foggy and frosty. Perfect.

I feel a bit bad about the hundreds of emails I have spammed you with concerning Jak's good and his bad behaviour.

You know just how much I love Jak but I am not really sure how you feel about him, having to read all my ups and downs for so long.

Anyway one day I will use all those emails to write a book or an article about how a Crazy Welsh type Collie changed my life!

I wonder what 2020 will bring?

xxxx

After Training

Early in 2020, I became able to take Jak on long walks to woodland close to my home where he could run free. Jak loved the running off the lead and exploring through the woods, sniffing out all sorts of interesting smells and sitting quietly with me watching the birds in the trees. This walk did not involve getting in the car, just pulling on wellington boots.

I always checked that I had plenty of treats and I put a tube of squeezy cheese in my pocket for unforeseen emergencies.

It felt bit bizarre that I took cheese with me as a back-up as I have always been allergic to cheese and avoided it my entire life. But, when there was a distraction that looked dangerous to Jak's behaviour, squeezy cheese was the only way to go! Jak sucked it out of the tube like a baby with a bottle and I can honestly say that squeezy cheese also made grooming easy, calm chew eating a reality and a short cut to getting Jak's ears to listen to me. Oh I am definitely much more interesting when I have the squeezy cheese tube in my hand.

The problem was that Jak still really disliked having the prong collar put on him and walking from the house. We no longer needed the distraction of the water bottle filled rucksack but without the prong collar Jak lunged at anything and everything barking and snarling ferociously.

To get to the woods we had to walk down a long lane and across fields to the woods. There were houses all down the lane that had dogs roaming loose or those that were behind gates that barked viciously at us. The loose dogs always ran around Jak and my feet and I could see that Jak was terrified. Because we went often he obviously recognised the dogs and did not react. But, everything about his body language screamed panic and fear.

It took about ten minutes to walk down to the woods and then we wandered together in the woods for at least an hour. There was a beautiful spot where a large pool of water met reeds and I found a 'secret' place where we could sit on the rocks and just gaze at nature.

We must have visited the woods sixty times or more and in all that time there were probably only six days that we met other people and dogs, and even then, we only had one incident of Jak looking aggressive. This was really the perfect place to learn more about Jak and his issues.

I did learn in the woods that if Jak was running free, off the lead for the entire hour, after about forty minutes he was tired and began doing crazy or dangerous things. This was the same over-excitement that I had seen when taking a toy on walks when Jak was younger. So I started alternating, putting Jak on and off the lead, until he was more than happy to walk beside me through the woods on adventures on the lead as well as free running.

This taught me that although Jak ran away from having his collar and lead on at home it was not the collar or lead itself that he disliked. Rather it was the having to go out into the wide world and walk on busy roads. I was more relaxed during these woodland days and I do believe that Jak felt that too. We really enjoyed this time together. It was a very blessed few months. We walked the woods through the winter, on muddy days, and on very wet days and in the snow.

This was much more how life with a Collie was supposed to be. But even though the time spent in the woods was really enjoyable, it was a real chore getting the collar and lead on Jak and walking to the entrance to the woods.

I had also started walking Jak along the canal towpath on some days of the week. On the whole he walked nicely. Seeing so far ahead on the straight path seemed to calm Jak and we did these towpath walks for many weeks.

Then, again, one day we had an event. For some reason, on this day, everybody seemed to be out walking their dogs. We had safely passed at least six when I saw Jak's body language change and saw him assume the 'stalking' position.

In front of us, at some distance, was a man walking a young Labrador type dog on a luminous extending lead. The dog was jumping about a bit and not well controlled. Jak even started growling quietly. I had not experienced this for at least a couple of months. We calmly carried on, there was nowhere to get a space between us. The approaching dog walker was on the canal side of the towpath.

As the dog came close to us Jak launched himself teeth showing, growling and snarling. I managed to hold him tight although I got another bite on my thigh. A few metres ahead an elderly man was walking with a smaller terrier type dog. Jak's body language was calm and I anticipated nothing. As the man drew adjacent to us Jak unexpectedly launched himself.

As I was not ready, the lead was loose in my hand, and Jak got right across to the elderly dog walker. The man leaped aside to get away from Jak and very nearly fell into the canal.

The incident was over in seconds. The man shouted a long tirade of insults at me and my dog ownership skills. I did feel that his anger was warranted and I was just very relieved that he had not fallen into the canal.

Although I have since walked many miles of canal towpath since that day as part of my work, Jak has stayed at home and I have missed him on my walks.

Jak and the Rabbit

It was a normal, everyday, field and woodland walk. As we walked down the stony lane to the fields, fishing pool and woods, it started to rain. Not heavy, but that fine drizzle that feels inconsequential but that leaves one sodden to the core. I was gloriously happy.

I love wearing wellington boots, the freedom to splosh through anything to get as muddy as muddy can be and to dance in the rain.

I am not sure that Jak shares my joy of the rain and mud. For a Collie, Jak is obsessional about being clean and it took him several rainy walks to get him to even step into a puddle. He still looks at his usually white tipped paws with incredulity when they are muddy and black. Thankfully, due to advice from Katy, we now have a bucket and cloth waiting for a post-walk routine followed by Jak being zipped up in a towelling bag until he is vaguely dry.

So, anyway, there we were in the squelchy field running and laughing (me, rather than Jak) and just generally wandering around in the great outdoors. Jak usually trailed around in my area keeping one eye on me and I sometimes tried to slip away unnoticed here and there to keep him attentive on the route I was taking.

We walked around the edge of a fishing lake then I went into the woods. There was silence. No Jak. This was strange. I retraced my steps and blew the gundog whistle. I could see Jak, he was showing great interest in something in the shallow flood water of the fishing pond. I walked a little closer, then took a deep shocked breath as I recognised it as something dead.

Thinking on my feet, I blew the whistle quickly and ran back into the field as fast as I could. Surely Jak would come. And, bless him, he did come.

Jak ran right up to me, sucked his squeezy cheese and looked at me slowly, directly, eye to eye, as if weighing something up. I could almost see his quick Collie brain whirring round.

Suddenly Jak ran at top speed back through the gate to the pond and in what seemed like seconds later he appeared carrying the limp, lifeless, droopy, leg waving, corpse he had plucked from the water. It was a deceased rabbit.

Jak ran directly at me. "No, No, No" I shouted and waved my arms frantically. To no avail, Jak was so proud of what he had managed to find that he wanted to jump all over me with it.

Now I am an animal lover, and a staunch supporter of the Small British Mammal, but I only like them alive. Dead things creep me out and I started to run from Jak to get away from the monstrous dead rabbit.

Game on! Wow this was the best game Jak had ever played. He chased and chased me. Now and then, he would put the rabbit down in the long grass and trot towards me as if the rabbit was gone then as I reached down to put his lead on he would, at the speed of light, grab the rabbit and start chasing me again.

What a movie clip it would have made. Me, alternatively screaming, running and waving my hands in the air. Even the squeezy cheese was no use to me. I was trapped in this field with a plotting dog and a dead rabbit trying to get me. My anxiety clicked in and all at once I was unable to see a way home.

I pictured myself walking home with Jak and the deceased rabbit. I considered running home and letting Jak follow but there were roads. No responsible owner would even think of doing that.

Almost an hour passed. I had lost a lot of calories, "maybe I would fit into those old jeans now," I pondered? What should I do? I couldn't stay here forever. The rain was now heavy and I was drenched.

I had never seen Jak so happy and obviously the rabbit had never had so much fun either. It was only me who was not enjoying this experience.

A sudden thought struck me and I phoned my husband, he always knew what to do when I was flummoxed. The phone was answered on about the sixth ring. It was rather inconvenient phoning at work, I did know that. But this was a terrible emergency.

I listened as the calm voice instilled hope in me that all would, eventually be well. As I listened, when the occasion arose that Jak had dropped the carcass I blew the whistle the accustomed five short loud blasts. It was only at the third time of blowing that the calm voice raised and said "and would you stop blowing that in my ear please?" It had not occurred to me that blowing the loud whistle repeatedly down the microphone of the mobile phone was a really bad idea.

Of course, eventually, we got home rabbit free and my hyperventilating slowed and this walk became a good story. I had loved seeing how happy Jak was playing this naughty game and it reminded me of the game he had played in the garden when he had only been with me for a couple of weeks but he had managed to snatch my knitted beanie hat off my head in the garden.

This extended game had certainly been very gross but Jak had been super happy. This incident had shown me that Chaseand 'I've got your things' were still activities that Jak liked to do most!

For the record, this was not the first time that my long suffering husband had needed to rescue me on this particular walk. Some weeks earlier, there was a lamb lost on the lane as we made our way up towards the road. The more we walked up the lane the nearer the road the lamb strayed. Eventually I called home and my husband walked down the lane thus sending the lamb back down towards the field rather than up to the road.

When I relayed the details of the dead rabbit game to Katy she was horrified, imagining that Jak had wanted to eat the dead rabbit. But for once, Jak had not been focussed on food and eating. He had been free doing something that he loved and he had been free from his anxieties.

Kitchen Games and Trick Training

One of the games that Jak and I had been playing together in the kitchen since Jak was neutered was dribbling the football. We played this with an indestructible Kong Jumbler ball. I dribbled the ball around the kitchen and Jak tackled me and tried to get the ball away from me. Obviously, as the ball has a handle that Jak can pick it up by, there was some Collie cheating right from the start.

But, a few weeks into the game, I discovered that my dribbling skills were increasing and Jak was watching me more carefully and planning his tackles better. The game became a real source of joy for us both and some good physical exercise for me too. We played it nearly every day, and still do. We can keep the game up for quite a while and I have become adept at pushing the ball through Jak's legs and getting back onto it before Jak has had chance to turn around and re-engage.

I needed to write this because there are so few areas in which I manage to outwit that pesky Collie! And I am sure that in the future Jak will be upping his footballing skills and I will be coming off second best here too.

One day after our usual dribbling, I had the idea to try and see if Jak could be a goalkeeper. I took the ball and made Jak sit in the doorway to his pen and he waited whilst I lined myself up and took shots. It only took a few attempts for Jak to get the gist of the game and so, here was another entertainment we had discovered.

Well, despite the fact that Jak could now walk nicely and ignore most dogs, unless they were misbehaving, Jak still really didn't like walks at all. He was always very relieved to get home.

I had told Jak repeatedly that it was very inconvenient for me that he did not enjoy walking as I originally got him to be my walking companion and I was still hoping for long distance hikes with him. Jak always listened very intently, looking like he understood every word I said, sometimes tipping his head on one side and looking really cute.

I also showed Jak other, really good dogs, walking with and cuddling up to their owners on television programmes. But Jak didn't seem to care! He remained my crazy Jak.

Another thing that I had noticed was that Jak also liked problem solving. If he dropped a toy down the back of the crate he took ages working out how to move the crate in order to retrieve it. Jak could open and shut the crate door and move other things out of the way first so that the door would open. I thought this was very clever.

This was obviously how Jak worked out how to open all the different doors of our house, from either side, and to unbolt his crate from the inside. I felt if I could find some puzzle solving activities for Jak he would be very happy indeed. In fact if I could harness these great talents Jak possessed and get him a job or a movie deal I am sure he would be a star. It is a pity that he is so reluctant to share his talent with the world.

Another day I decided to try to play Hide and Seek with Jak using a toy rather than the treats that books suggest. I chose a tiny blue dinosaur cleverly called 'Dino' for this game. It took Jak about ten minutes to learn that after I had hidden Dino in the conservatory he was free to go and find it. Almost straight away I had to start closing the curtains separating the conservatory from the kitchen and ensure that Jak stayed on the kitchen side because I could see Jak actively cheating! He was watching me closely as I placed the toy and finding it immediately.

After two attempts behind the curtain where, Jak did sit beautifully, I discovered that he was still cheating by carefully peeking through the curtains so that he knew exactly where to go to find Dino.

I rejoiced that this was the first game that did not require treats other than the kitchen football that we had been playing for some months now. This meant that the enjoyment of the game was payment enough. Great news.

Another plan that evolved around this time in an effort to get Jak more exercise was to try out a dog walking arm that fastened onto my bicycle. I put this attempt off for quite a few weeks as I was totally unsure of how it would go. I was very afraid that Jak would hare off in pursuit of something and a terrible accident would ensue.

Eventually, I took the plunge and rode my bicycle around our enclosed car park. It turned out that Jak did love running alongside the bicycle. It only took him a couple of minutes to work out that when I gave him a warning I was turning a corner and he had to watch the front wheel carefully.

To date, Jak and I have not cycled outside the private car park as I am not sure what would happen when we passed a person or especially a dog. But I am hopeful that this type of exercise may become something that Jak can enjoy more fully in the future.

Of course, I will be truly cross if I have to change my long distance hiking plans for long distance cycling ones. After all, who isit that is in charge here?

Jak's repertoire of tricks grew steadily over the months. He could 'play dead' when I shot a toy pistol at him. He could jump onto even high bar stools and sit looking regal. And then there was the start of the sheepdog commands training.

Many months ago, when I wondered if Jak would make a sheepdog, I learned the first commands of 'Away' and 'Come by'. These commands send the dog out to run around the sheep in either a clockwise (Come By) or anti-clockwise (Away) movement. I decided to try and get Jak to learn these commands indoors with the use of the dining table.

A couple of days after starting doing this for a few pieces of kibble Jak understood what I was asking him to do. After he had learned to 'round up' the dining table we moved onto drying racks and other household items.

Then, I started getting Jak to lie down to command in the middle of the circling movement. Then we worked on Jak balancing my movements around the object as a sheepdog would around a pen.

I had hoped that in the future Jak would be able to herd yoga balls as in the sport of Treibball. I would then buy a goal net for him to herd them into. However, on purchasing the perfect yoga ball I found out that although Jak didn't mind running around it or even, very briefly, touching it with his nose, Jak was scared of the ball whenever it wobbles or moves.

This, obviously, was a bit of a setback to herding the ball into a goal, but I remain optimistic. We will keep practicing and perhaps Jak will get brave enough to give it a go. It will give me great pleasure if Jak will be able to focus on a sheepdog type activity sometime in the future. Of course I have wondered about owning ducks, or a couple of sheep. But I think my next door neighbours really have enough to contend with.

I am anticipating that over the months and years to come Jak will continue enjoying learning new tricks and games. I am hopeful that we will keep finding activities that we can share and enjoy together.

I am very sad that Jak can only really share these successes with my friends and work colleagues by me filming them and putting them on Facebook as Jak still gets very panicky when there are visitors to the house. We will keep working on these issues together. I would love Jak to be able to relax when we have visitors. Or even better, to come to work with me and show off his skills.

I would like to think that in the future I will be able to visit Katy without Jak running amok over the furniture, barking as people enter the house, or molesting Grandma but I do think that Jak and I may still be a few years off that good behaviour yet even though Jak has calmed down so much at home.

Covid 19. Update April 2020

The outbreak of Covid 19 provided an important piece of the puzzle that solved a lot of Jak's behaviour issues that I had struggled with. In the week leading up to the 'Stay at Home' campaign Jak had only been out to the woods once for a walk due to my poor health.

As we entered the United Kingdom's version of 'lockdown' I decided not to walk Jak outdoors at all and to try doing lots of training with him at home and in the garden. Over the first ten days of being at home all day every day something magical happened. Jak and I got to understand each other better.

Now that there was no daily stress of a forced walk that Jak did not enjoy, he started to trust me more and we started having funny little interludes each day where we seemed to be able to communicate with each other over small things, toys, Jessie and her behaviour, and feeding routines.

Jak relaxed so much that he became able to lie on the sofa in the evenings with me. Only by invitation. I dared not grant him the freedom of the lounge. He would totally relax, even resting his head on my legs, and snoring. I had never seen behaviour like this. I loved it and I started staying up much later. This was one of the two big things I had originally wanted from my own dog. Company in the lounge in the evenings.

I remembered that when Jak was younger I used to desperately hang out for that time of night when Jak could go in his crate and I could collapse in a heap of stress and exhaustion. How much better was this time of cuddling on the sofa each evening relaxing together?

It seemed to me that what Jak had been trying to tell me over the last eighteen months was that he just could not cope with walking outdoors. He was just too scared.

I remembered Jak's very first training camp when his trainer had told me that Jak was lacking in confidence and that this was causing much of the aggressive behaviour on the lead. Was this time, where we just spent quiet days together, building Jak's confidence? Would there be a further change in Jak's ability to go on walks after this? Only time will tell.

I also realised that dealing with Jak's high energy levels when he was not being walked daily was easier than I had thought it would be. I remembered that in some of my most early research, when I had read a farmer's blog on the internet, I had read that many farmers moan that their sheepdog would rather lie on the sofa than work for them! Perhaps this was the type of sheepdog that Jak aspired to be?

So, I am currently spending a lot more time training at home in order that Jak can be a happy, cuddly companion at home even if this means that I will have to go hiking alone.

I have not given up on Jak walking with me in the future. I am hoping that after lots of trust building together it may just be possible to start at the beginning again. Perhaps with Jak just fastened on the harness I use with the bicycle rather than with anything round his neck. It may just work, particularly when Jak is even more mature than now. It would be great if I could train Jak to look forward to having his harness on for treats and short walks rather than him trying to hide when I get his lead out which we have had for many months now.

I often wondered whether if I were just to pack up my back-packing tent and rucksack, pick up Jak's lead and go hiking, really hiking, for a month or more, whether Jak and I would get it together and Jak would stop worrying about walking. I am currently still too afraid to try just in case Jak is super anxious every day and gets worse rather than better. But perhaps one day we will go.

During this time of enforced staying at home I have had the opportunity to sit in the kitchen, writing this book and watching Jessie and Jak cavort around the kitchen together. Jessie can only manage about ten minutes of 'playing with Jak' action before she heads off to the safety of her protection pen. It really is great to see them doing some play bowing at each other and Jak being able to restrain himself and play nicely.

I sometimes go over and over the journey that Jak and I have taken over the last eighteen months or so. I wonder about all the things we have tried and failed at. All the moments where Jak was afraid, or distressed. And I wonder if I could have dealt with it all better. But I have to acknowledge that Jak has been a very special case. Most dogs love being outdoors enough to overcome any fears they have.

If I had not tried the walking with the prong collar and the dog rucksack, I would not have been able to walk Jak in fun places and learn that no matter how great or exciting the walk was Jak was still out of his comfort zone in the wide world. Also all of the advice regarding Collies accentuates how much physical exercise they need and that a lack of exercise usually results in behavioural issues.

There was no reason for me, or any of the trainers, to think that Jak was any different and, of course, when Jak is relaxed in the fields and can stop constantly anticipating danger, as the incident with the dead rabbit proved, Jak does love running and jumping freely.

I had also worried that by trying new types of training I may have confused Jak but, I am now finding that all these months later, I am now able to use, very successfully, some of those techniques that I was shown way back in the beginning of the journey. These seemed to have had no effect on Jak whatsoever at the time but are now coming into their own.

I have learned a huge number of skills that, now Jak is really listening, we can work on together.

My plan for when life returns to normal, is that I will pay to rent an enclosed and private dog walking field at least once a week where Jak can arrive in the car and run to his heart's content. We may possibly even do some agility training there.

Also if I can find a safe place to extend our cycling together we will be doing that too. Will we ever get to do that long distance hike together? I will have to wait and see.

How much better our future looks now than when I could not understand Jak and when he could not tell me just how afraid he was.

Encouragement

Today if you have read this book because you have a dog who is breaking your heart, you love him or her and have invested so much into their life and yet you cannot enjoy life with them please take heart.

My advice is firstly, find a Katy who can read your long and despairing emails and uplift you in your day to day struggles.

Secondly, keep trying different trainers if you can afford to do so, until you can find one who can help with your dog's specific issues. Jak spent training time with, in total, six different trainers and training settings. It took all of those differing training experiences in order to find out that Jak needed the methods Hannah at Canissimo Dog Training and Behaviour excels in. This enabled Jak to walk amongst people and dogs on the lead properly, and reliably, for the first time. By watching Jak's body language and gauging how he was feeling on his walks it was then possible to assess how big the issue was for Jak. Therefore, I could finally see just how stressed Jak really was outside of the house.

All of this was needed in order to completely understand Jak's outdoor walking issues that had been constantly escalating since his first few walks. It has been a long and painful journey for both of us, and obviously, the problems are not as yet resolved.

I am also comfortable with admitting that Jak and I have nothing like made it yet. There are still behavioural issues I see in Jak that need investigation and more research and training. There are still things that I need to read up on before I can begin to sort current, and potentially future, problems out.

It would be great if I became able to change Jak's reactions to make life easier for both of us in the future.

It has felt like a very long road.

But if you were to see Jak and I playing football together, or performing tricks, you would see a beautiful, happy dog who loves spending time with me….and, obviously, lounging around on the sofa with me a lot!

I hope, and indeed I firmly believe, that when Jak is an older adult dog our life will be easier, fun and even a walk may be a daily pleasure. If I did not keep believing in that possibility I would not have been able to get this far.

So, may I encourage you, let your mind dwell on the issues and problems that you have resolved not the ones which still lie ahead like jagged rocks in a tempestuous sea.

Enjoy the moments, no matter how fleeting, when your dog looks at you, really looks into your eyes, and you can see that dog you are shaping for the future.

If necessary, write down every happy moment in a diary so that you can see that being the owner of your dog is not a miserable, depressing situation, it is merely a journey that you both need to take to get to where you want to go!

Katy said "I reckon the Jak story would make a good sermon, perhaps you should include it. A lesson to all about understanding others, well dogs at least".

I do hope, and I pray, that Jak's story will help you and your dog with your story. Amen.

Books Featuring Naughty Jak

Baby Jak Explores:
A read it Together Photo Puppy Book

Baby Jak Explores is a
photo journey of the early
weeks of puppy
Kaiser Jackaroo Redboy III.
A cheeky, and very naughty,
Sheepdog puppy.

Baby Jak Explores

A Read it Together Photo Puppy Book

By ABLang

Baby Jak gets Bigger:
A read it Together Photo Puppy Book

Baby Jak gets Bigger is a photo
journey of puppy
Kaiser Jackaroo Redboy III.
A cheeky, and very naughty,
Sheepdog puppy. In this book Baby
Jak gets big enough to be really
naughty!

Baby Jak Gets Bigger

A Read it Together Photo Puppy Book

By ABLang

Books Featuring Naughty Jak

Baby Jak has Friends:
A read it Together Photo Puppy Book

Baby Jak Has Friends is the third photo book about Kaiser Jackaroo Redboy III. A cheeky, and very naughty, Sheepdog. In this book Jak introduces some of his friends!

Baby Jak Has Friends

A Read it Together Photo Puppy Book

By ABLang

All available from Amazon.co.uk

These books contain photos of Jak from 8 weeks old to 18 months. Also some photos of the friends that Jak has been able to play with.

The books are aimed at reading together for an adult and pre school child.

Why not keep up to date with Jak and his adventures by visiting Jak's Facebook Page

Naughty Jak

https://www.facebook.com/JakCollie/

Appendix

Trainers

Zoe Phillips Tudful Dog Academy Merthyr Tydfil
https://www.facebook.com/tudful/

ADK9 Trained Dogs Chesterfield
admin@adk9.co.uk

Gilliana Elliott www.packleadertechniques.co.uk

HannahPrice Cannissimo Dog Training
https://www.facebook.com/canissimodogtraining/

Vicki Sykes at www.bordercollies.co.uk

There are also resources and help available at:

Freedom of Spirit Trust Border Collies who Rescue,
Rehabilitate and Rehome Collies.
www.fostbc.org.uk

Farming Courses

Kate's Country School (For Farming Days)
http://www.katescountryschool.co.uk/

Printed in Great Britain
by Amazon